PENGUIN  CLASSICS

THE LITERATURE OF
JAPANESE AMERICAN INCARCERATION

FRANK ABE is lead author of the graphic novel *We Hereby Refuse: Japanese American Resistance to Wartime Incarceration* and a finalist in creative nonfiction for the Washington State Book Award. He wrote, produced, and directed an award-winning PBS documentary, *Conscience and the Constitution*, on the largest organized camp resistance, and with writer Frank Chin helped create the first Day of Remembrance in Seattle in 1978.

FLOYD CHEUNG is a professor of English Language and Literature and American Studies at Smith College. Coeditor and contributor to *Recovered Legacies: Authority and Identity in Early Asian American Literature*, he has worked on the recovery of H. T. Tsiang, Sadakichi Hartmann, Kathleen Tamagawa, Munio Makuuchi, and others.

Together, Frank, Floyd, and Greg Robinson won an American Book Award from the Before Columbus Foundation for editing *John Okada: The Life and Rediscovered Work of the Author of No-No Boy*.

The Literature of Japanese American Incarceration

Edited with an Introduction by
FRANK ABE
and
FLOYD CHEUNG

PENGUIN BOOKS

PENGUIN BOOKS

An imprint of Penguin Random House LLC
penguinrandomhouse.com

LIBRARY OF CONGRESS CATALOGING-IN-PUBLICATION DATA
Names: Abe, Frank, editor, writer of introduction. |
Cheung, Floyd; 1969– editor, writer of introduction.
Title: The Literature of Japanese American Incarceration / edited with
an introduction by Frank Abe and Floyd Cheung.
Description: [New York] : Penguin Books, 2024.
Identifiers: LCCN 2023045373 (print) | LCCN 2023045374 (ebook) |
ISBN 9780143133285 (paperback) | ISBN 9780525505044 (ebook)
Subjects: LCSH: American literature—Japanese-American authors. |
Japanese Americans—Forced removal and internment, 1942–1945—Literary collections. |
LCGFT: Fiction. | Poetry. | Essays. | Autobiographies. | Personal correspondence.
Classification: LCC PS508.J36 L58 2024 (print) | LCC PS508.J36 (ebook) |
DDC 810.9/8956073—dc23/eng/20240208
LC record available at https://lccn.loc.gov/2023045373
LC ebook record available at https://lccn.loc.gov/2023045374

Printed in the United States of America
1st Printing

Set in Sabon LT Pro

Contents

Registration and Segregation

Volunteers and the Draft

Resegregation and Renunciation

PART III: AFTER CAMP

Resettlement and Reconnection

Repeating History

Preface

The literature in this volume presents the collective voice of a people defined by a specific moment in time: the four years of World War II during which the United States government expelled resident aliens and its own citizens from their homes, farms, and businesses, and incarcerated more than 125,000 of them in American concentration camps, based solely upon the race they shared with a wartime enemy.

Bowing to popular fear after planes from the Imperial Japanese Navy bombed the U.S. naval base at Pearl Harbor in Hawai'i on December 7, 1941, President Franklin D. Roosevelt and Congress denied Americans of Japanese ancestry any individual hearings or other due process before authorizing their mass removal and imprisonment. Government officials registered and numbered them by family, then subjected the captive people to a series of administrative orders, including a second registration with a loyalty questionnaire, a segregation based upon the results of that questionnaire, the military conscription of young men from the camps, and the offer of voluntary renunciation of American citizenship. By its own latter-day admission, the government had no military need for the mass exclusion—acknowledging that it was driven by a mixture of race prejudice, war hysteria, and a failure of political leadership—rendering the three-year incarceration that followed just as unnecessary as it was wrong.

This anthology reclaims and reframes the writing produced by the people targeted by these actions. You will hear many voices telling a shared story. It's the story of the struggle to retain personal integrity in the face of increasing dehumanization.

The selections favor writing that is pointed rather than poignant. Not all are polished, but each conveys a central truth. We present these writings chronologically so that readers can trace the continuum of events as the incarcerees experienced it.

This collection contains a mix of prose and poetry, of fiction and of nonfiction drawn from essays, memoirs, and letters, all anchored by the key government edicts that incite the action. The first two sections feature pieces written at the time or later in retrospect. The postwar section includes the work of the children of the camps, the third- and fourth-generation descendants who look back across the divide of time and memory to grasp the meaning of mass incarceration and its long-term consequences to themselves and the nation.

In place of familiar selections readily found elsewhere, this volume recovers pieces that have been long overlooked on the shelf, buried in the archives, or languished unread in the Japanese language. The number of new translations from the Japanese we present testifies to one of the long-term effects of camp: the loss of language and culture due to regulation, suppression, and the ongoing stigma of acknowledging any affinity to Japan. These selections focus on the incarceration of Japanese Americans by the U.S. government and as such do not address the incarceration of Japanese Canadians or the kidnapping of Japanese Latin Americans for a hostage-exchange program.

Our commentary for this volume avoids euphemisms historically used to describe the mass exclusion and incarceration, but these terms are left intact where they appear in the texts. "Evacuation" is a word best applied to humanitarian removal for safety from natural disasters such as hurricanes and floods. "Internment" legally applies only to the detention of those designated as enemy aliens, while the confinement of citizens and of resident aliens who were denied the opportunity of naturalized U.S. citizenship is properly called an "incarceration." Euphemisms for the camps include "colony," "project," and "relocation center." By definition, these were concentration camps—places where large numbers of a persecuted minority are confined under armed guard—and were regularly referred to as such at the time; they are distinct from the extermination centers or death camps of the Third Reich.

The original language of the texts is also preserved where it includes racial slurs and dismissive stereotyping, which reflects the ethnic prejudices and class hierarchies of the time but which some readers will find upsetting. Where the occasional profanity occurs, it is retained to convey the impact intended by the writer. Ellipses indicate excisions to enhance readability. Where chapters or excerpts do not come with a heading, we have taken the liberty of adding a title drawn from the text itself.

Many of the voices in this volume are those of protest against incarceration. Some are those of accommodation. All are authentic. Together they form an epic narrative with a singular vision of America's past, one with disturbing resonances with the American present.

FRANK ABE *and* FLOYD CHEUNG

The Literature of Japanese American Incarceration

PART I

BEFORE CAMP

The first emigrants from Japan to Hawai'i and the United States in the late nineteenth and early twentieth centuries call themselves the Issei, or first generation in America. Unlike immigrants from Europe, however, the Naturalization Act of 1790 bars those from Asia from applying for American citizenship, reserving that privilege to "free white persons." Alien land laws prevent the Issei from owning land in many western states, and the federal Immigration Act of 1924 closes the Pacific border to further arrivals. This lack of status empowers their children, the Nisei, or second generation, who are born on U.S. soil with birthright American citizenship under the Fourteenth Amendment ratified in 1868. To assert their standing and promote their assimilation, young Nisei professionals organize their own Japanese American Citizens League (JACL), to which the Issei cannot belong.

ARRIVAL AND COMMUNITY

In the earliest known Japanese American graphic narrative, *The Four Immigrants Manga*, educated young men feel triumphant upon their "Arrival in San Francisco," only to find they must take manual jobs. When confronted by white workers threatened by their competitive labor in "The Turlock Incident," Henry Kiyama satirizes the desire of the immigrants to stand on rights they do not have. Issei like them help build the American West working alongside migrants from China and elsewhere to cut timber, harvest crops, and carve through rock to lay railroad tracks. By 1940, the Nisei make up nearly two thirds of the Japanese American population, and in "Whither Immigrants," journalist Ayako Ishigaki can already see the children breaking from the language and culture of Japan and their parents. She shows how the Issei avoid racial conflict by congregating in thriving Japantowns and Little Tokyos, leaving them unknown to the American mainstream, the "other." However, everyone has a name and a place in Toshio Mori's "Lil' Yokohama," which celebrates individual identities in both generations within the wholeness of a Japanese American community that will soon all be lost.

ARREST AND ALIEN INTERNMENT

Japanese Americans are as shocked as anyone by the attack on Pearl Harbor. "Those Airplanes Outside Aren't Ours," exclaims the Issei protagonist of Shelley Ota's novel *Upon Their Shoulders*, squarely identifying where his loyalty lies. On the mainland, artist Kamekichi Tokita experiences the attack that Sunday as news on his radio, and like many Issei he blames the conflict on the U.S. embargo of oil to Japan and fears the consequences of war between the militarists in the land of his birth and the people of the nation where he's lived for just as long and where he's raised five children. He begins a diary that notes the Japanese calendar year as "1941 (Showa 16)," or the sixteenth year of the reign of the then-current emperor.

On the Monday after Pearl Harbor, college freshman John Okada sees that his own professor and classmates cannot look him in the eye. His anxiety and confusion as a Nisei hardens into resolve with "I Must Be Strong," published anonymously on December 11 in the University of Washington *Daily*.

The Rev. Bunyu Fujimura of Salinas is among the first to face "Arrest" as the army and the FBI take into custody and interrogate 5,500 Issei on the West Coast and in Hawai'i, separating families and leaving wives and children to deal with frozen bank accounts, vandalism, and death threats. Fujimura believes he faces execution and boldly defies an agent who interrogates him about spying for Japan. In Fujiwo Tanisaki's short story newly translated for this volume, a Nisei son describes how "They Took Our Father Too"; from the internal evidence, the father is most likely taken to the Tuna Canyon Detention Station, a former Civilian Conservation Corps (CCC) camp near Los Angeles.

The men arrested are shifted to a succession of army and Justice Department internment camps where they are further grilled by alien enemy hearing boards. Schoolteacher Otokichi Ozaki and newspaper publisher Yasutaro Soga from Hawai'i are among those who compose *tanka*—short songs of thirty-one syllables each—to grapple with the humiliation of their arrest, their movement to the mainland, and the fear that leads at least one fellow inmate to take his own life. At Fort Missoula, Montana, where he shares a barracks with German and Italian prisoners of war, business manager Iwao Matsushita writes to his wife in Minidoka, Idaho, "I Can't Bear to Be Stigmatized as 'Potentially Dangerous,'" and offers strategies for clearing his name and securing his release.

COOPERATION AND REFUSAL

Despite the lack of any verifiable acts of sabotage or espionage by Japanese Americans, the White House capitulates to the threats perceived by the army, racial demagoguery from West Coast congressmen, and pressure from agricultural business owners who covet the lands richly cultivated by the Issei. With an executive order numbered 9066, President Roosevelt authorizes his secretary of war to prescribe military areas from which any or all persons can be excluded. Nowhere does the order mention Japanese Americans by name, but its meaning is clear. Four days later in San Francisco, publisher James Omura testifies to the lack of due process at a hearing of the House Select Committee Investigating National Defense Migration, commonly known as the Tolan Committee, and puts the question directly to the lawmakers: "Has the Gestapo Come to America?"

The JACL steps into the leadership vacuum left by the arrest of the Issei. JACL's first paid executive secretary, Mike Masaoka, describes his "Decision to Cooperate" with the government as one made to prevent bloodshed in the streets and demonstrate the loyalty of the Nisei. Having taken this position, Masaoka also issues statements waiving the right to protest removal and opposing any constitutional test cases in court.

The head of the army's Western Defense Command, Lt. Gen. John DeWitt, claims military necessity to order the removal of all Japanese Americans and resident aliens from the western half of Washington, Oregon, and California, and the southern part of Arizona. Soldiers nail 108 localized Civilian Exclusion Orders to buildings and utility poles under the stark headline, "Instructions to All Persons of Japanese Ancestry"; excerpted here is Order No. 33, addressed to the Little Tokyo community of Los Angeles. Until this moment, most Nisei accept that their Issei parents may be detained but believe that their status as citizens will protect the American born. They are sickened and angry to see that racial ancestry is the only criterion for removal, with the order applying to both resident aliens and to what the poster now euphemistically calls "non-aliens." The orders direct each family to register their names and receive a five-digit family number, with one week to report to a designated pickup spot. Aside from the alien hearing boards, the government grants no hearings, trials, or questionnaires to the exiles to determine individual loyalty, despite the Fourteenth Amendment guarantee of equal protection and due process before any deprivation of life, liberty, or property.

Only now do families scramble to dispose of homes, farms, and businesses to comply with army orders. University of Washington student Gordon K. Hirabayashi, however, cannot in good conscience obey first a military curfew and then the exclusion order, as both are enforced solely on the basis of race, as he explains in "Why I Refuse to Register for Evacuation." And on the day that he is "Kicked Out of Berkeley," Charles Kikuchi wonders in his diary how families on the street in distress can still appear to smile for photographers as they board buses for the assembly center at the Tanforan Racetrack.

Arrival and Community

1.

HENRY (YOSHITAKA) KIYAMA

ARRIVAL IN SAN FRANCISCO
and
THE TURLOCK INCIDENT

Arrival in San Francisco

The Turlock Incident

Sign on hanging lamp: *Japanese Inn*

AYAKO ISHIGAKI

(as Haru Matsui)

WHITHER IMMIGRANTS

In the morning, while writing my column, I looked out of the window of the newspaper office upon the street of "Little Tokyo," and thought of the hidden sorrows of my compatriots. In California the notion that the Japanese are an inferior race is still prevalent. Often Japanese do not even have the liberty to rent and live in houses outside of certain districts. When they go to a barber shop or a drugstore, they are sometimes treated rudely, and even refused service. The sensitive feelings of those who live in a strange country are easily wounded by such slight things as a look or a manner of speaking. It is in order to avoid the hard, lonely feeling of having their pride trampled upon, that the Japanese cling together as closely as they do, and do not mix in American life. The street which the farm wife looks forward to visiting is not the Broadway of Los Angeles, but the minutely-built, elaborate and confusing street of "Little Tokyo." Some Japanese people grow nervous even when they walk along a street among American people, and their hearts become heavy. A whole family going on a happy picnic will not choose the beautiful mountain and seashore spots which surround Los Angeles, but will go to one particular spot where Americans do not go. For fear of the treatment they might receive, some Japanese women I met had not taken one step out of the Japanese section, although they had lived in Los Angeles for over ten years.

Even though Japanese immigrants have cultivated the wild land to green, have laid down railroads and cut and brought down lumber from the mountains, and have lived several decades in this country, they cannot become American citizens. When they consider the fact that they have no right to own or even to lease the land which they have cultivated, they turn to the thought that their children, born here, will have the privileges of American citizenship, denied to them. They hang all their hopes on their children.

Most of these people who migrated to this strange land to break the new ground of their fate, were without education; and they have been so busy working, smeared with mud, that they have had no time to learn even a word of English. Whenever they gaze at their rough chapped hands, they hope their children will not suffer in the same way. It is the common desire of Japanese parents to give their children the education which will provide new vistas and opportunities in life, and often they endure great hardship in order to raise the necessary funds.

But these children in whom the parents thus rejoice gradually grow away from their elders as they approach maturity. It is the parents' pleasure to see the tall stature of the younger generation, and their manner of walking—lively, long-legged like the Americans—as they go along kicking the sidewalks. But it is a grave worry to see that the children, not only in appearance, but also in manner of thinking, have become American. The eyes of the children no longer shine at the story of the Japan which the parents long for. The second generation, grown up in American atmosphere, cannot understand the Japanese customs which their parents cherish. Difference in thought between parents and children may be common in every age and in every land; but in this case, with the widely dissimilar background of Japan and America, the difference is infinitely greater.

As the second generation in Los Angeles comes of age, there are many instances where a broad, deep channel is dug between children who insist upon their independence and parents who cannot understand them. In many families, the parents speak Japanese and the children English; and the lack of a common language and the impossibility of expressing more subtle feelings, further strains the relationship. Often children who are graduated from universities find no positions open to them, and they are obliged to labor at back-breaking work like their parents—a bitter disappointment. Members of the second generation, even though they are American citizens, find themselves pushed toward social ostracism because their skin is yellow; and they tend to accept discrimination as their fate.

Looking down on the street of "Little Tokyo," I thought of all these things.

TOSHIO MORI

LIL' YOKOHAMA

In Lil' Yokohama, as the youngsters call our community, we have twenty-four hours every day . . . and morning, noon, and night roll on regularly just as in Boston, Cincinnati, Birmingham, Kansas City, Minneapolis, and Emeryville.

When the sun is out, the housewives sit on the porch or walk around the yard, puttering with this and that, and the old men who are in the house when it is cloudy or raining come out on the porch or sit in the shade and read the newspaper. The day is hot. All right, they like it. The day is cold. All right, all right. The people of Lil' Yokohama are here. *Here, here*, they cry with their presence just as the youngsters when the teachers call the roll. And when the people among people are sometimes missing from Lil' Yokohama's roll, perhaps forever, it is another matter; but the news belongs here just as does the weather.

Today young and old are at the Alameda ball grounds to see the big game: Alameda Taiiku vs. San Jose Asahis. The great Northern California game is under way. Will Slugger Hironaka hit that southpaw from San Jose? Will the same southpaw make the Alameda sluggers stand on their heads? It's the great question.

The popcorn man is doing big business. The day is hot. Everything is all set for a perfect day at the ball park. Everything is here, no matter what the outcome may be. The outcome of the game and the outcome of the day do not matter. Like the outcome of all things, the game and the day in Lil' Yokohama have little to do with this business of outcome. That is left for moralists to work on years later.

Meanwhile, here is the third inning. Boy, oh boy! The southpaw from San Jose, Sets Mizutani, has his old soupbone working. In three innings Alameda hasn't touched him, not even Slugger Hironaka. Along with Mizutani's airtight pitching, San Jose has managed to put across a run in the second. The San Jose fans cackle and cheer. "Atta-boy! Atta-boy!" The stands are a bustle of life, never still, noisy from bytalk and cries and the shouts and jeers and cheers from across the diamond. "Come on, Hironaka! Do your stuff!" . . . "Wake up, Alameda! Blast the Asahis out of the park!" . . . "Keep it up, Mizutani! This is your day! Tell 'em to watch the smoke go by." . . . "Come on, Slugger! We want a homer! We want a homer!"

It was a splendid day to be out. The sun is warm, and in the stands the clerks, the grocers, the dentists, the doctors, the florists, the lawnmower-pushers, the housekeepers, the wives, the old men sun themselves and crack peanuts. Everybody in Lil' Yokohama is out. Papa Hatanaka, the father of baseball among California Japanese, is sitting in the stands behind the backstop, in the customary white shirt—coatless, hatless, brown as chocolate and perspiring: great voice, great physique, great lover of baseball. Mrs. Horita is here, the mother of Ted Horita, the star left fielder of Alameda. Mr. and Mrs. Matsuda of Lil' Yokohama; the Tatsunos; the families of Nodas, Uyedas, Abes, Kikuchis, Yamanotos, Sasakis; Bob Fukuyama; Mike Matoi; Mr. Tanaka, of Tanaka Hotel; Jane Miyazaki; Hideo Mitoma; the Iriki sisters; Yuriko Tsudama; Suda-san, Eto-san, Higuchi-san of our block . . . the faces we know but not the names: the names we know and do not name.

In the seventh, Slugger Hironaka connects for a home run with two on! The Alameda fans go mad. They are still three runs behind, but what of that? The game is young; the game is theirs till the last man is out. But Mizutani is smoking them in today. Ten strike-outs to his credit already.

The big game ends, and the San Jose Asahis win. The score doesn't matter. Cheers and shouts and laughter still ring in the stands. Finally it all ends—the noise, the game, the life in the park; and the popcorn man starts his car and goes up Clement.

It is Sunday evening in Lil' Yokohama, and the late dinners commence. Someone who did not go to the game asks, "Who won today?" "San Jose," we say. "Oh, gee," he says. "But Slugger knocked another home run," we say. "What again? He sure is good!" he says. "Big league scouts ought to size him up." "Sure," we say.

Tomorrow is a school day, tomorrow is a work day, tomorrow is another twenty-four hours. In Lil' Yokohama night is almost over. On Sunday nights the block is peaceful and quiet. At eleven thirty-six Mr. Komai dies of heart failure. For several days he has been in bed. For fourteen years he has lived on our block and done gardening work around Piedmont, Oakland, and San Leandro. His wife is left with five children. The neighbors go to the house to comfort the family and assist in the funeral preparations.

Today which is Monday the sun is bright again, but the sick cannot come out and enjoy it. Mrs. Koike is laid up with pneumonia and her friends are worried. She is well known in Lil' Yokohama.

Down the block a third-generation Japanese American is born. A boy. They name him Franklin Susumu Amano. The father does not know of the birth of his boy. He is out of town driving a truck for a grocer.

Sam Suda, who lives down the street with his mother, is opening a big fruit market in Oakland next week. For several years he has been in Los Angeles learning the ropes in the market business. Now he is ready to open one and hire a dozen or more men.

Upstairs in his little boarding room, the country boy has his paints and canvas ready before him. All his life Yukio Takaki has wanted to come to the city and become an artist. Now he is here; he lives on Seventh Street. He looks down from his window, and the vastness and complexity of life bewilder him.

But he is happy. Why not? He may succeed or not in his ambition; that is not really important.

Sixteen days away, Satoru Ugaki and Tayeko Akagawa are to be married. Lil' Yokohama knows them well. Sam Suda is a good friend of Satoru Ugaki. The young Amanos know them. The Higuchis of our block are close friends of Tayeko Akagawa and her family.

Something is happening to the Etos of the block. All of a sudden they turn in their old '30 Chevrolet for a new Oldsmobile Eight! They follow this with a new living-room set and a radio and a new coat of paint for the house. On Sundays the whole family goes for an outing. Sometimes it is to Fleishhacker Pool or to Santa Cruz. It may be to Golden Gate Park or to the ocean or to their relatives in the country. . . . They did not strike oil or win the sweepstakes. Nothing of the kind happens in Lil' Yokohama, though it may any day. . . . What then?

Today which is Tuesday Lil' Yokohama is getting ready to see Ray Tatemoto off. He is leaving for New York, for the big city to study journalism at Columbia. Everybody says he is taking a chance going so far away from home and his folks. The air is a bit cool and cloudy. At the station Ray is nervous and grins foolishly. His friends bunch around him, shake hands, and wish him luck. This is his first trip out of the state. Now and then he looks at his watch and up and down the tracks to see if his train is coming.

When the train arrives and Ray Tatemoto is at last off for New York, we ride back on the cars to Lil' Yokohama. Well, Ray Tatemoto is gone, we say. The folks will not see him for four or six years. Perhaps never. Who can tell? We settle back in the seats and pretty soon we see the old buildings of Lil' Yokohama. We know we are home. . . . So it goes.

Today which is Wednesday we read in the *Mainichi News* about the big games scheduled this Sunday. The San Jose Asahis will travel to Stockton to face the Yamatos. The Stockton fans want to see the champs play once again. At Alameda, the Sacramento Mikados will cross bats with the Taiiku Kai boys.

And today which is every day the sun is out again. The housewives sit on the porch and the old men sit in the shade and read the papers. Across the yard a radio goes full blast with Benny Goodman's band. The children come back from Lincoln Grammar School. In a little while the older ones will be returning from Tech High and McClymonds High. Young boys and young girls will go down the street together. The old folks from the porches and the windows will watch them go by and shake their heads and smile.

The day is here and is Lil' Yokohama's day.

Arrest and Alien Internment

4.

SHELLEY AYAME NISHIMURA OTA

THOSE AIRPLANES OUTSIDE AREN'T OURS

That Sunday morning Taro had been taking an early morning stroll in his garden, as was his custom before breakfast. He was never a late sleeper, and he loved the garden in the early morning hush. He fed the birds that alighted on the feeding trough and walked up and down the flagstone path, admiring a bloom, picking a dry leaf here and there, adjusting a support that had fallen from his prize-winning dahlia, Golden Queen, and breathing deeply of the cool morning breezes that were blowing in from the sea. He sat down under the trellis of red roses and looked toward the sky, marveling at the peace and serenity of the Hawaiian morning.

Suddenly his eyes grew sharp as he saw squadrons and squadrons of airplanes spanning the sky. Then he relaxed and smiled in reassurance. It is the usual routine, he thought, lighting his pipe. He puffed in contentment and closed his eyes. He had often seen this practice of the army and navy, admiring the graceful flight. As he looked again he saw the glint of the sun on the markings. To his horror he saw the emblem of the Rising Sun. He jumped to his feet and rushed into the house, the blood pounding in his veins. He yelled at Haruko, who was still in bed. She came running out, with her robe trailing after her.

"I can't believe it," he cried out. "The fools!" He covered his ashen face with his hands and weakly sat down.

"What are you talking about?" asked Haruko in alarm, noting his shaking hands.

"We're at war!" Taro shouted to her. "Those airplanes outside aren't ours. They're from Japan." He leaped to his feet and turned on the radio and heard the excited voice of the radio announcer filling the stillness of the room with the awful news: "Bombs are falling on Pearl Harbor." The words trailed off, telling the bitter story of unpreparedness.

Taro stared at the dazed Haruko. A hundred things clicked in his mind, with an ominous meaning, a pattern shaping. Isolated incidents began to form a definite picture. He, too, had been fooled. He had always thought that Japan had enough on her hands with the war in China and would not possibly pick on America.

"So," he swallowed with difficulty, taking a deep breath, "that's why the Japanese banks closed their books earlier than usual." He had idly speculated on the move, but the businessman in him would not attach significance to the act, save that it was just a new policy. Yes, because he could not think of a war with America. He groaned in despair. The whole thing had seemed ridiculous to him, knowing the economic structure of Japan. Purely braggadocio on Japan's part, he thought.

"The *baka*," he said under his breath. "The fools took the gamble."

He jumped to his feet and blurted to Haruko, his face white, "Do you know what this makes us!" He stared at her. "Enemy aliens!" Every line in his face was taut. He sank to a chair by the window and covered his drawn face with his shaking hands. A shudder ran through him. "An enemy alien—" Over and over the words ran in his mind. He bit his lips—he who prided himself on being an American.

True, he did not have the status of citizenship, but he believed that the day would come when America would correct this injustice by amending the act which forbade citizens of Japan to become American citizens. He had prided himself on being a respected taxpayer, but now, because he was not a citizen, he would be classed with those plotting fiends who had planned this attack.

He was defeated. He saw himself imprisoned for the duration of the war, saw his property confiscated, saw all the years of work destroyed—years of working toward a dream of personal and economic freedom. Like a child he wept, his tears running down his pale cheeks.

Haruko put a hand on his trembling shoulder. "Don't, Taro," she entreated. Her words rang out clear. "I'm sure that it is not going to be as bad as you think. After all, we have friends who believe in us, trust us, in spite of the blood in our veins."

Taro lifted his face and smiled faintly. He wished that he could believe it. But what was war but a mounting hysteria that pushed aside cool judgment and common sense? He had seen what men could do in the heat of passion, and this was war—he shook his head and covered his face with his shaky hands.

Would discrimination raise its ugly head in the hysteria of war? Taro did not deny the existence of a dual world in Hawaii, a privileged one for the haoles and a restricted one for the Orientals.

Slowly, like a man doomed, he went to the telephone and called Jerry's number, hurling the news at him.

"Here, drink this coffee," Haruko suggested hopefully, appearing at his side. Anxiously she watched him.

Taro drank the hot liquid slowly, his thoughts milling in his mind. He ate the fruit Haruko had placed before him, ate it, because he knew that there was a great deal to be done before the day ended. He brought his brows together determinedly. Enemy alien or not, he would offer his services to the country which had nurtured him and his family.

He pulled on his coat and searched in his pockets for the car keys. Haruko took them from the kitchen drawer and handed them to him. She stood there quietly by his side, saying not a word. At a moment like this, she knew that silence was golden.

He paused briefly at the door and glanced at Haruko, who was still standing in the kitchen anxiously watching him. He smiled reassuringly. "I'll be all right. Don't worry." She nodded gravely.

Down the pebbled pathway he went to the garage. He jumped into the car and started it, and backed out of the garage slowly and with great deliberation, the simple mechanical act freeing his mind from its dazed state. Almost immediately he felt new physical energy flowing in him. He had a plan now, and he was going to execute it as best he could.

The attack, he sensed, was at its height. He could see the aerial fighting, and the clouds of smoke billowing up in the distance. He sensed that Pearl Harbor must be hard hit; that smoke in the sky like a thick blanket was testimony to the amount of damage the enemy had done.

Traffic was a torrent of confusion. Every vehicle seemed headed toward Pearl Harbor, horns screeched, and cars darted in and out. Taro gritted his teeth in exasperation. He wanted to be on his way, for it would be just a matter of time before order would be restored, and of course, an enemy alien wouldn't be permitted to travel freely.

He thought for a minute the police officer on the corner would hail him to a stop, but the brown-faced man recognized him and shouted, "Bad business." Taro waved his hand and nodded.

He parked his car, slammed the door, and hurried up the steps. Someone shouted to him, but he paid no attention and ran into the elevator.

A voice at his elbow called his name, and he looked up. It was his old friend, Chester Philips, now aged and gray. The two shook hands, and their grasp was warm and understanding.

Philips said thickly, "Bad business, Taro, but we are in this together." Taro nodded gratefully, realizing that Philips, an old-timer, a *kamaaina*, spoke for the haoles who had come to know and respect the Japanese.

Taro got off at his floor and waved to Philips. In a daze he walked toward the receptionist at the Bureau of Investigation. The girl eyed him coolly and he steeled himself, knowing he was likely to meet such reception often in the days to come. "Get used to it," he scolded himself. "There'll be people putting a label upon you, hating you for your blood."

5

KAMEKICHI TOKITA

1941 (SHOWA 16)

*Translated by Haruo Takasugi and
Naomi Kusunoki-Martin*

1941 (Showa 16)
December 9 (Tues.)

I really fear the mob mentality. There was a blackout in our area last night. Friedlander's Jewelers downtown forgot to turn off their neon sign and was vandalized. I heard there were a few other similar incidents downtown, too.

The owner of the restaurant on the street corner, a friendly Caucasian lady, visited us this morning to make sure we were okay. She advised us not to have cash in our house. She offered to keep our money in a safe inside her restaurant. That would be one way to deal with the current situation. Even though she is a Caucasian, she came to check on us because she was deeply concerned about our well-being. This is very encouraging. She left a piece of paper with her restaurant's number and her home phone number and told us to call her if anything should happen.

The tone of the radio broadcasts sounded a bit different. I found out that Germany and Italy had declared war against the United States. Actually at this point, their declaring war against the United States was assumed to be inevitable because the U.S. had begun criticizing Germany and blaming Hitler for all this mess.

Seven at night, the U.S. President issued a proclamation to the nation. Maybe because I was calmer, or maybe because I didn't quite understand his speech, I listened to his proclamation relatively calmly. His speech contained some difficult words here and there, but I listened very intently and found the overall message easy to grasp. In addition, the speech sounded powerful enough to raise the nation's morale.

From the point of view of the United States, I could see that some of his arguments are reasonable. He said that without warning during the last few years, Germany had occupied first Czechoslovakia, then Poland, Belgium, France, and Denmark in succession. Italy took over Ethiopia without warning, and Japan took over Manchuria.

From Japan's or Germany's or Italy's viewpoint, however, each must have its side of the story. If Great Britain and the United States had found a way to provide Japan, Germany, and Italy with an appropriate amount of resources, this war would never have happened. Intelligent people could have resolved these issues by considering the fair distribution of benefits. This is the most fundamental issue. Yet, for the past few years, people from every nation seem to have forgotten all about it, focusing only on fighting. I wish Great Britain and the United States had cared a little more for these three relatively poor countries. Japan, Germany, and Italy have been earnestly trying to get their attention for several years, but Great Britain and the U.S. deliberately shut out their voices and wouldn't listen. That was quite unreasonable. If only there had been a great politician in Great Britain or the U.S. who had figured out a way to supply them with enough resources to live moderately, and to bring about some benefits for their own countries as well, such a big war would have never broken out.

Anyhow, my mind has become somewhat calmer and people in town seem to be coping with the situation. The radio broadcast has returned to a somewhat normal tone that is more pleasant to listen to. With Germany's participation in this war, the United States may have shifted some of its focus away from Japan.

The local Japanese papers will stop delivering temporarily tomorrow. I'm going to miss them.

6.

JOHN OKADA

(as Anonymous)

I MUST BE STRONG

I know now for what war I was born.
Every child is born to see some struggle,
But this conflict is yet the worst.
For my dark features are those of the enemy,
And my heart is buried deep in occidental soil.
People will say things, and people will do things,
I know they will, and I must be strong.

I dread the thought of having to leave home each day,
The thought that I must continue as naught has happened,
For clouds will hang where the sun was bright.
Everyone will smile, but what of their thoughts
As they gaze on one whose eyes are so black?
People will say things, and people will do things,
I know they will, and I must be strong.

7

BUNYU FUJIMURA

ARREST

Translated by Ken'ichi Yokogawa

Early in the morning of February 11th, 1942 (February 10th in the United States), to commemorate Empire Day, the anniversary of the day Emperor Jimmu first ascended the Japanese throne, the Japanese Imperial Army took Singapore.

That same morning, someone knocked softly on the door of our bedroom on the second floor of the Salinas Buddhist Temple. Rubbing the sleep from my eyes, I opened the door to find two men, one in his sixties and the other in his thirties.

"We are from the FBI," the older man said in Japanese, and showed me his badge.

While I was getting dressed, the older man went through all my books, which were, of course, all in Japanese. The younger man carefully checked my clothes.

Reverend and Mrs. Koyo Tamanaha, who were sleeping downstairs, were also awakened. We were then ordered to go to the residence next door, where Reverend Hoshin Fujikado and his family were living.

I noticed over ten policemen keeping close watch over both the front and rear gates of our temple. Perhaps this precaution was taken because they knew Reverend Tamanaha had a fifth-degree black belt in judo.

Not long after, the milkman delivered our milk. After asking permission, I began heating it, but before I could get any down my throat, we were ordered to get into the car, so I ended up not having anything for breakfast.

Reverends Fujikado, Tamanaha and I were brought to the police station where a group of newspaper photographers were waiting. We were blinded by flashes from their cameras. My wife tells me that I usually have a stern expression, but for some reason, I smiled just as the cameras clicked.

That night, the photographs they took were published in newspapers all over the country.

The caption under the photograph in the *San Francisco Call-Bulletin* was typical, "Reverends Fujimura, Fujikado, and Tamanaha of the Salinas Buddhist Temple caught in FBI net. Reverend Tamanaha was a former police chief in Tokyo."

Life magazine showed a photograph of the gong that had been lowered from its place in the tower, and under it stated that the "three Buddhist priests . . . smiled courteously while being arrested."

Later, when I was sent to Bismarck in North Dakota, Mr. Yoshito Fujii told me that a young *nisei* in Seattle saw that photograph and said, "Reverend Fujimura has guts to be able to smile in a situation like that. He is a true Buddhist!"

I was led to wonder how differently the same photograph is perceived by different people.

At any rate, we were imprisoned in the basement of the Salinas jail. Many others were also there, with one exception, all Japanese members of our Salinas Buddhist Temple. The exception was a Filipino who lived in a cheap boarding house managed by a Japanese named Sensho. He was undoubtedly mistaken for a Japanese because to the police, "they all look alike."

I had missed breakfast and lunch, but when dinner time arrived, we were taken to a restaurant. The restaurant featured only American food with which I was then unfamiliar, so I was in a quandary about what to order. I finally ordered a T-bone steak that I had heard much about, but had never tasted. That was how, thanks to the United States government, I was introduced to this delicacy.

Reverend Tamanaha and I began to be questioned during the middle of the night.

Reverend Fujikado was not questioned.

The person who questioned me was the elderly FBI man in charge. He spoke Japanese quite well.

First question: With a frightening look on his face, he asked, "Are you a spy?"

Answer: "No."

Second question: "Did you come to the United States because of orders from the Emperor of Japan?"

Answer: "No."

Third question: "Have you ever met the Japanese Emperor?"

Answer: "No. I have worshiped the Emperor, but I have never met him."

Fourth question: "The Japanese Emperor and the Spiritual Leader of your Buddhist denomination, Otani *Monshu*, are cousins. You are responsible to this Otani *Monshu*, so there is no reason why you should not have received orders from the Japanese Emperor."

Answer: "It is true that Otani *Monshu* and the Emperor of Japan are cousins, but it is ridiculous to think that I received any orders from the Emperor of Japan."

Fifth question: "How many different denominations are there in the Buddhist teaching?"

Answer: "Don't ask such irrelevant questions. I am the one who knows about Buddha-dharma here . . ."

Sixth question: "The Salinas Buddhist Temple has only 300 members. Three ministers for such a small temple seems excessive. Further, you are Reverend Tamanaha's superior even though he is older than you. Why is that?"

Answer: "Do you mean to tell me that no one working in Washington D.C. is older than President Roosevelt?"

"I am the one who is questioning you," the FBI agent said. "There is no need for you to ask me questions!"

Seventh question: "Why does the Salinas Buddhist Temple entertain Japanese-American soldiers stationed at Fort Ord?"

Answer. "Japanese-American soldiers are American citizens so the American government should thank us for entertaining them."

Eighth question: "Are you a Japanese Naval officer?"

Answer: "How can a skinny person like myself be a Japanese Naval Officer? (I was quite thin in those days, so much so that I was called *pakkai*, which in Japanese refers to bones with little meat.) This should be apparent even to you."

In addition to the above questions, I was asked about the relationship between the Nishi Hongwanji headquarters in Kyoto and the Buddhist Mission of North America (which is presently known as the Buddhist Churches of America), about my education, my personal history, finances, and many other things. The questioning lasted until dawn.

As I was being questioned, it occurred to me: I am the first minister in the Buddhist Mission of North America to be arrested. How I answer these questions may result in all ministers of the mission being placed in the situation I am now. Now is the time for me to live up to the words of Shinran *Shonin*, the founder of my Jodo-Shinshu Buddhist tradition, who wrote:

> My indebtedness
>   to the Buddha Amida's
>   Great Compassion
> Must be repaid,
>   Though I
>   Be crushed . . .

I must not answer in a cowardly fashion, I thought. Now is when I must sacrifice myself. Now is the time for me to repay my debt to the dharma. I determined to answer all the questions truthfully, but courageously. . . .

The authorities seem to have already decided that I am a spy, I thought, and regardless of how I proclaim my innocence, it is highly unlikely that they would even care to listen. And since we were at war, I will undoubtedly be executed. My country (which then was still Japan), my parents, brothers and sisters, my wife, friends—there was no one on whom I could rely. When I thought about this, the following words of Shinran *Shonin* came to mind: "All things in this impermanent world that is like a burning house, are false and vain, completely without truth. Only the Nembutsu is true."

8

FUJIWO TANISAKI

THEY TOOK
OUR FATHER TOO

Translated by Andrew Way Leong

Even after the war started, they continued the project of cleaning city hall. Workers, precariously perched on long planks suspended by ropes, had been washing the dirt-stained walls by hand. The upper portion of the tower was now a pure white, stretching up into the blue sky. The trees surrounding the building were just beginning to sprout their first young buds, and a soft breeze blew gently through the clear air. All signs pointed toward a light and pleasant spring, but the shouts of the newspaperman and the news on the radio drifting out of a nearby bar . . . all of those sounds stung the ears of Kenji, a boy with a Japanese face. With these sounds gathering, lurking behind his back, pressing down upon him, there was no hope of feeling bright and cheerful.

Kenji was in junior high, and his walk back from school took him through the frightening streets of Filipino Town, where Filipinos would idle along the sidewalks or loiter by the storefronts. It gave him the creeps just to walk through that place. He would always tuck his bundle of books tightly under his arm and rush through as quickly as he could.

The moment he made it through, he was in Japantown. More and more stores were closing by the day, and the Japanese people on the streets all seemed to be in a hurry, dark expressions clouding their faces.

All sorts of furniture and household goods had been brought out onto the sidewalks, and here and there loud-talking Jewish people were haggling for better deals. There was something gross about just seeing their fat bellies.

Scraps of paper littered the front of the Asia Emporium, which had finished its closing clearance sale. The inside of the store was dark, with nothing left but dust. The window display was empty, but a few people had gathered to read a sign that was posted there. The sign was in Japanese.

One of the old men raised his voice as he read. He looked at the map displayed on one side and muttered, "Looks like it's not our turn just yet. I wonder when we'll have to go . . ."

"We'll go whenever we end up going," snapped the man standing next to him. Another man, tall and ungainly, drew a breath from his unlit pipe.

"No need to rush. Wherever we're going, it's nowhere nice. I'm happy staying right here, even if it's not for long." The tall man laughed. Everyone laughed.

Today, it seemed, another exclusion zone had been announced. The area on the map marked out with the red-penciled line had grown once again.

Kenji returned home. He opened the door and saw the desolation. Most of the furniture was gone. Even the carpet had been rolled up and sold off. It was quiet, as if no one was home, and the last remaining items—an antique electric stove, a broken radio—had been pushed into a corner. His father had been busy making crates, well into the night, to store their valuables. "Sooner or later we're going to get the evacuation order, so best be prepared," he would say. He was taking care of things. That's why there was a pile of half-finished crates in the parlor, and scraps of wood, a hammer, a saw, a sewing box. . . . Kenji sat down on one of the crudely constructed crates, and strange and half-formed apprehensions played out before his eyes, one after another.

Just then, he overheard the voice of his mother. She was on the telephone upstairs. "Yes. The FBI came this morning around ten. . . ." "No." "We knew this would happen eventually, so we were prepared." Kenji stood up with a start, realizing that his father must have been taken. Then he sat back down. At dinnertime, and other times, his father would often say, "They're coming to get me any day now." The image of Father's face as he would say this, half joking, floated into Kenji's mind. His mother had already packed his things into a suitcase so that he would be ready to go at a moment's notice. Kenji could imagine, with brilliant clarity, how his small-statured father would have been holding that suitcase when the tall white men came to get him. The tears that Kenji had been holding back began to stream down his face.

"I'm home!" His older sister Shizuko was at the door. Kenji stood up and wiped away his tears. His sister took one look at him and asked, "What's wrong? Why are you crying?" His mother came down the stairs. She had a grave expression on her face, and seemed a little pale, but did not say a word. Shizuko tried to say something, but broke down in tears instead.

It took about a week, after asking for some help from a kind white person, to find out where Father was being held. It turned out that he was pretty far away. He was in a CCC camp thirty miles out, so they had to ask around the neighborhood for someone who could drive the family's car. Kenji's mother observed aloud, to anyone listening, "The car still has payments left. The company's going to come for it any day now. Good thing we still have it." Everyone was talking about what they imagined Father's life was like in the camp. Kenji didn't say out loud what he was thinking, that they were probably giving his father a really hard time. Soon enough, his sister said what Kenji was only thinking. Mother, appearing as if she had expected this all along, said, "Shizuko, that's enough. Stop thinking those kinds of thoughts." She turned away and looked out the window. It was clear and sunny, an unusually warm day for that time of year. "This would have been a nice place for a picnic," she said, almost whispering. Kenji thought that even if it was going to be picnic season soon, for Japanese like him, happy things like picnics were something far away now, lost in the distance.

The road turned sharply as they went deeper into the mountains, and they soon arrived at a place where crowds of visitors were waiting in long lines. The camp was at the bottom of a ravine, surrounded by barbed wire. There were also visitors trying to speak through the metal fences. People who had said their goodbyes were turning back, their eyes red from trying to wipe away their tears. The first impression was one of overwhelming sadness.

"Let's try not to cry," Kenji's sister whispered into their mother's ear.

Their names were called earlier than they expected. Kenji was walking closely behind his mother and sister as they made their way to the metal fence, but he could not see his father. Someone called out his father's name. Then he was there. He was looking from side to side, trying to find his family, and when he finally saw them he pushed his way through the people in front of him and pressed up against the fence. Kenji's mother began to speak. His sister wiped her face with her handkerchief. *Speak English!!* a guard yelled out. *All right*, his father said. It was in that moment, as his father was turning to look up at the guard, that Kenji realized how pale his father's face was, how dark and sunken his eyes were. Kenji's mother looked down at the scraps of paper she had prepared, and while continuing to speak in Japanese, threw in loud *and*s and *but*s to make it sound like she was speaking in English. Through this difficult method, she was able to get across all that needed to be said. Two minutes was hardly enough time to describe all that had happened in the last week, but the important details were exchanged nevertheless. Next was Shizuko, who quickly said, "We brought you some clothes and other things. It sounds like they'll give them to you once they clear inspection." Kenji wanted to say something as well, but he had no idea what he should say. His father asked him, "You still studying hard?" Kenji just nodded. His face was so stiff he couldn't even smile. The guard came between them. Father told them not to worry, it would all be fine. Shizuko was sobbing. The people waiting behind them could see everything, so Kenji tried not to cry.

As they walked to the car, they turned to look back at the camp, and they saw a man, a man who could have been Father, waving his hat high above his head. It was hard to tell if it was him through their tears. They waved back. Their feet grew heavy. When they got into the car and looked back again, they could no longer see the man. There was only the metal fence, gleaming in the sharp, white sunlight.

9.

OTOKICHI OZAKI

(as Muin Ozaki)

FORT SILL INTERNMENT CAMP

Translated by Jiro Nakano and Kay Nakano

I bid farewell
To the faces of my sleeping children
As I am taken prisoner
Into the cold night rain.

∾

Sailing on the same ship—
The son,
A U.S. soldier;
His father,
A prisoner of war.

∾

A wretching anguish rises
As the number "111"
Is painted
On my naked chest
In red.

10.

YASUTARO SOGA

(as Keiho Soga)

SAND ISLAND AND SANTA FE INTERNMENT CAMPS

Translated by Jiro Nakano and Kay Nakano

Like a dog
I am commanded
At a bayonet point.
My heart is inflamed
With burning anguish.

∾

A fellow prisoner
Takes his life with poison.
In the evening darkness,
Streaks of black blood
Stain the camp road.

∾

The barren wasteland
Raged by sand storm,
I weep for my friend
Who sleeps there alone,
Eternally.

11

IWAO MATSUSHITA

I CAN'T BEAR TO BE STIGMATIZED AS "POTENTIALLY DANGEROUS"

Translated by Akimichi Kimura

Dec. 7, 1942

Dear Hanaye,

On this anniversary date, it was decided that I'm to be interned. It was quite unexpected and regrettable. You'll probably be terribly disappointed having waited a lonely year with hopeful expectations, but please don't cry. Keep your chin up. Let's think of the families of soldiers who are fighting in the heat of the tropics or in the cold snow, what they must be feeling.

There are fortunes and misfortunes in this world. The Bible says, "One shall be taken and one will be left behind." We can't expect that all things will be meted out fairly. Eight out of ten who have been sent here are to be interned, so that's a small consolation, but I can't blame you for being disappointed when in fact there were some that were released. When I compare my circumstances with those that were released, I can't help being very perturbed.

You, as well as a host of others, know that I haven't done anything that would harm America. I stand before God innocent of all guilt. It's said that a setback is sometimes a blessing in disguise. The fact that I couldn't be released to go to Minidoka may be God's divine will, and we won't know whether it'll be for the best until later. As in the hymn, "Where He leads me I will follow," let us accept His command and pray that His blessings will be upon us.

The reason for my internment, according to the Attorney General, was that I was "potentially dangerous to the public safety." I am keenly disappointed that the sincerity of my love of America in my appeal had not been accepted. Since there's no use dwelling in the past and "crying over spilt milk," let's consider some future options.

1. Rehearing. This is held if, at the initial hearing, you were not able to fully state your case, or if substantial evidence has been uncovered and submitted to the Hearing Board with an affidavit of an influential individual who can vouch for your character and background, and if the Board deems your case has sufficient merit to warrant a rehearing. Generally, unless you have extremely convincing evidence, permission for a rehearing is usually denied. In fact, there's a case where an appeal made several months ago has never been acknowledged.

I've had my say in my first hearing, so I've nothing else to add. I felt so good after the hearing, it was like the sky clearing. At this date I've nothing to submit, and the only affidavit I can probably get is from Mr. Griffin, so I don't think I have a chance going this route. I heard, though, that there've been some that have gone to your camp as a result of a rehearing. Do you know anything about it?

2. Reconsideration. This isn't a formal procedure, but there's been a case where a wife of an internee had an important American friend write a convincing affidavit saying that while her husband is interned he is of no use to the United States, but he would be useful should he be released. She petitioned Washington, and as a result her husband's sentence was rescinded and he was paroled. I'm thinking

about doing the same. Especially in my case, the Hearing Board had recommended release but the Attorney General had stated that the evidence at his disposal warranted internment. Now, I don't believe any evidence exists that would be detrimental to me. Even if there were thought to be, I'm sure it could easily be explained. However, there may be a matter of interpretation. For example, if I picked up a stone unthinkingly for no reason, and that was construed as my intent to throw it, there's no defense. Accordingly, I wonder if we shouldn't make a direct appeal to the Attorney General with a joint petition from you and me, and possibly one from an American friend.

3. To request a transfer to a family camp. This has to be done in any case if my internment status is changed to parole and I am not permitted to return to the center. According to your letter I received today, there's already an inquiry being done at your camp, so we should definitely submit our request without delay.

If the plan doesn't agree with you, the problem is whether to go with (2) and ask for a rehearing and make an effort to be released to the center, or seek one of the other options.

For myself, I can't bear to be stigmatized as "potentially dangerous," so I propose to petition for a rehearing and at the same time request our joint tenancy. The point is we need to be together as soon as possible. You may know of families in your camp with internment returnees who can relate their experience, or you may have good ideas of your own. Please give this careful thought and give me your reply. I doubt if the internees left here will be suddenly be transferred to another site.

A couple, three days ago, we had a visit from an official from the U.S. State Dept. asking us about our treatment. I told him I'm most distressed by being separated from my family. He said, "Please be patient and bear it awhile, we're already working on that problem."

There's been a disturbance at the Arizona's Poston Relocation Center, and there also was an ugly incident yesterday at California's Manzanar Camp. We're saying how troublesome those camps were, and we'd be better off in a family camp.

This letter will take the place of three, so you won't hear from me the rest of this week. Please give my thanks to Doc for all he's done for us. I'm deeply indebted to him. Our reunion was postponed, but I feel I can see the sunshine behind the dark clouds. Let's take care of our health and pray to God that we can be together again soon. You mentioned the people who have been so kind and helpful while you were ill. Please give them my personal thanks and regards.

Sayonara, Iwao

Cooperation and Refusal

EXECUTIVE ORDER

AUTHORIZING THE SECRETARY OF WAR
TO PRESCRIBE MILITARY AREAS

WHEREAS the successful prosecution of the war requires every possible protection against espionage and against sabotage to national-defense material, national-defense premises, and national-defense utilities . . .

NOW, THEREFORE, by virtue of the authority vested in me as President of the United States, and Commander in Chief of the Army and Navy, I hereby authorize and direct the Secretary of War, and the Military Commanders whom he may from time to time designate, whenever he or any designated Commander deems such action necessary or desirable, to prescribe military areas in such places and of such extent as he or the appropriate Military Commander may determine, from which any or all persons may be excluded, and with respect to which, the right of any person to enter, remain in, or leave shall be subject to whatever restrictions the Secretary of War or the appropriate Military Commander may impose in his discretion. The Secretary of War is hereby authorized to provide for residents of any such area who are excluded therefrom, such transportation, food, shelter, and other accommodations as may be necessary, in the judgment of the Secretary of War or the said Military Commander, and until other arrangements are made, to accomplish the purpose of this order. . . .

I hereby further authorize and direct the Secretary of War and the said Military Commanders to take such other steps as he or the appropriate Military Commander may deem advisable to enforce compliance with the restrictions applicable to each Military area hereinabove authorized to be designated, including the use of Federal troops and other Federal Agencies, with authority to accept assistance of state and local agencies. . . .

/s/ Franklin D. Roosevelt

THE WHITE HOUSE,
    February 19, 1942.

9066

12

JAMES OMURA

HAS THE GESTAPO
COME TO AMERICA?

TESTIMONY OF JAMES M. OMURA, EDITOR AND PUBLISHER,
CURRENT LIFE, SAN FRANCISCO, CALIF

Mr. OMURA: It is doubtlessly rather difficult for Caucasian Americans to properly comprehend and believe in what we say. Our citizenship has even been attacked as an evil cloak under which we expect immunity for the nefarious purpose of conspiring to destroy the American way of life. To us—who have been born, raised, and educated in American institutions and in our system of public schools, knowing and owing no other allegiance than to the United States—such a thought is manifestly unfair and ambiguous.

I would like to ask the committee: Has the Gestapo come to America? Have we not risen in righteous anger at Hitler's mistreatments of the Jews? Then, is it not incongruous that citizen Americans of Japanese descent should be similarly mistreated and persecuted? I speak from a humanitarian standpoint and from a realistic and not a theoretical point of view. This view, I believe, does not endanger the national security of this country nor jeopardize our war efforts. . . .

We cannot understand why General DeWitt can make exceptions for families of German and Italian soldiers in the armed forces of the United States while ignoring the civil rights of the Nisei Americans. Are we to be condemned merely on the basis of our racial origin? Is citizenship such a light and transient thing that that which is our inalienable right in normal times can be torn from us in times of war? We in America are intensely proud of our individual rights and willing, I am sure, to defend those rights with our very lives. I venture to say that the great majority of Nisei Americans, too, will do the same against any aggressor nation—though that nation be Japan. Citizenship to us is no small heritage; it is a very precious and jealous right. You have only to look back on our records in social welfare and community contributions to understand that.

May I ask the committee members if any or all of you are acquainted with the Nisei? I believe that much of this distrust of citizen Japanese is based on ignorance. It would seem more compatible in the sense of fair play and justice that we should not be prejudged and that racialism should not be the yardstick by which our loyalty is measured. Our words, in current times, have no meaning, and so I ask you to examine our records, for there I believe that to a large measure, if not necessarily so, lies the true determination of our oft-questioned loyalty.

It seems to me that we are less fortunate than our alien parents. They, at least, are subjects of Japan and are entitled to recourse and redress through the Japanese Government. Not so is our case. We are but children of destiny—citizens by birth but citizens in virtually name only.

13.

MIKE MASAOKA

with Bill Hosokawa

DECISION TO COOPERATE

Late in February, even as the Tolan Committee continued its hearings, Kido and I were summoned to Western Defense Command headquarters in the San Francisco Presidio. We were ushered into the presence of General DeWitt, a short, stocky, gray-haired man with the three stars of a lieutenant general on his shoulders. DeWitt was surrounded by a bevy of lesser officers, all cold and stern. He did not introduce them. DeWitt made a brief statement making it clear that we had been called in to hear what the Army had to say, not for discussion or negotiation. With that he left the room.

Another officer broke the news. In a few days the Western Defense Command would issue Public Proclamation No. 1 announcing that "all persons of Japanese ancestry"—we were referred to as "aliens" and "nonaliens"—would be required to get out of the western half of California, Oregon, and Washington and the southern one-third of Arizona. The Japanese Americans would be urged to move out "voluntarily." If "voluntary" departure didn't work, the alternative would be transfer to temporary havens until the government could map the next move. It was obvious no one had any idea what that would be. But there was no doubt that the Army intended to proceed without delay; the removal of 115,000 men, women, and children, citizens and aliens alike, voluntarily or otherwise, would begin just as soon as arrangements could be made.

I heard all this in utter disbelief. I cannot remember ever feeling so desperately let down. What we in moments of doubt had feared might happen was about to take place, and there was nothing more we could do to try to prevent it. There was no more room for argument or reason, only the cold reality of military orders. On top of it all, the Nisei were being lumped together with enemy aliens. We had been prepared for drastic restrictions on the freedom of the Issei generation. But we had remained confident in the sanctity of our rights as citizens. I felt I had failed JACL and its members. What made it even worse was that the generals now were asking JACL to cooperate with them—to cooperate like Judas goats—in the incarceration of our own people. I gagged at the thought.

But in my desperation I could see another side. If mass evacuation was inevitable, the Army's request also confronted JACL with the responsibility to help minimize the pain and trauma of the ordeal ahead.

For the moment, Kido and I could not go beyond saying that we represented only our membership and that we had no authority or right to speak for the entire Japanese-American community. Even as representatives of JACL the decision as to its role was too important to be made by just the two of us. We asked for and received permission to call a conference of league leaders to discuss our response.

Kido and I left the Presidio in silence, but that was a prelude to many agonizing discussions about principles involved, the leadership obligations to the people that we had assumed involuntarily, and the new obligations the Army was asking us to accept. What an anomalous position we were in. Our government was asking us to cooperate in the violation of what we considered to be our fundamental rights. The first impulse was to refuse, to stand up for what we knew to be right.

But on the other hand there were persuasive reasons for working with the government.

First of all was the matter of loyalty. In a time of great national crisis the government, rightly or wrongly, fairly or unfairly, had demanded a sacrifice. Could we as loyal citizens refuse to respond? The answer was obvious. We had to reason that to defy our government's orders was to confirm its doubts about our loyalty.

There was another important consideration. We had been led to believe that if we cooperated with the Army in the projected mass movement, the government would make every effort to be as helpful and as humane as possible. Cooperation as an indisputable demonstration of loyalty might help to speed our return to our homes. Moreover, we feared the consequences if Japanese Americans resisted evacuation orders and the Army moved in with bayonets to eject the people forcibly. JACL could not be party to any decision that might lead to violence and bloodshed. At a time when Japan was still on the offensive, the American people could well consider us saboteurs if we forced the Army to take drastic action against us. This might place our future—and the future of our children and our children's children—as United States citizens in jeopardy. As the involuntary trustees of the destiny of Japanese Americans, Kido and I agreed that we could do no less than whatever was necessary to protect that future. I was determined that JACL must not give a doubting nation further cause to confuse the identity of Americans of Japanese origin with the Japanese enemy.

The officers had made it clear to us that we could cooperate or they would do it the Army way. Anxious to avoid panic, the military did not make that threat public, nor were we in a position to do so. Only when the evacuation was well under way did Colonel Karl R. Bendetsen, who has been described by the Army's official historian as the "most industrious advocate of mass evacuation," reveal in a blood-chilling speech to the Commonwealth Club of San Francisco that he had been prepared to complete the evacuation "practically overnight" in an emergency.

Reluctantly, we concluded there was no choice but to cooperate. We talked over the decision with friends and advisers, who, once over their shock, agreed we had no other choice. The few Issei community elders who hadn't been imprisoned counseled cooperation.

INSTRUCTIONS
TO ALL PERSONS OF
JAPANESE
ANCESTRY

Living in the Following Area:

All of that portion of the City of Los Angeles, State of California, within that boundary beginning at the point at which North Figueroa Street meets a line following the middle of the Los Angeles River; thence southerly and following the said line to East First Street; thence westerly on East First Street to Alameda Street; thence southerly on Alameda Street to East Third Street; thence northwesterly on East Third Street to Main Street; thence northerly on Main Street to First Street; thence northwesterly on First Street to Figueroa Street; thence northeasterly on Figueroa Street to the point of beginning.

Pursuant to the provisions of Civilian Exclusion Order No. 33, this Headquarters, dated May 3, 1942, all persons of Japanese ancestry, both alien and non-alien, will be evacuated from the above area by 12 o'clock noon, Pacific War Time, Saturday, May 9, 1942. . . .

The Following Instructions Must Be Observed:

1. A responsible member of each family, preferably the head of the family, or the person in whose name most of the property is held, and each individual living alone, will report to the Civil Control Station to receive further instructions. This must be done between 8:00 A. M. and 5:00 P. M. on Monday, May 4, 1942, or between 8:00 A. M. and 5:00 P. M. on Tuesday, May 5, 1942.

2. Evacuees must carry with them on departure for the Assembly Center, the following property:

    (a) Bedding and linens (no mattress) for each member of the family;

    (b) Toilet articles for each member of the family;

    (c) Extra clothing for each member of the family;

    (d) Sufficient knives, forks, spoons, plates, bowls and cups for each member of the family;

    (e) Essential personal effects for each member of the family.

All items carried will be securely packaged, tied and plainly marked with the name of the owner and numbered in accordance with instructions obtained at the Civil Control Station. The size and number of packages is limited to that which can be carried by the individual or family group.

3. No pets of any kind will be permitted.

4. No personal items and no household goods will be shipped to the Assembly Center.

5. The United States Government through its agencies will provide for the storage, at the sole risk of the owner, of the more substantial household items, such as iceboxes, washing machines, pianos and other heavy furniture. Cooking utensils and other small items will be accepted for storage if crated, packed and plainly marked with the name and address of the owner. Only one name and address will be used by a given family.

6. Each family, and individual living alone will be furnished transportation to the Assembly Center or will be authorized to travel by private automobile in a supervised group. All instructions pertaining to the movement will be obtained at the Civil Control Station.

Go to the Civil Control Station between the hours of 8:00 A. M. and 5:00 P. M., Monday, May 4, 1942, or between the hours of 8:00 A. M. and 5:00 P. M., Tuesday, May 5, 1942, to receive further instructions.

J. L. DeWitt
Lieutenant General, U. S. Army
Commanding

May 3, 1942

14

GORDON K. HIRABAYASHI

with James A. Hirabayashi and Lane Ryo Hirabayashi

WHY I REFUSE TO REGISTER FOR EVACUATION

As far as the Japanese American community was concerned, in terms of the norms of the 1940s, protesting was not a front-line activity, not even a backline option. The Japanese American Citizens League (JACL) was the big thing in the Japanese community. I knew the leaders, men like Jimmy Sakamoto and Bill Hosokawa. They were working on opposite things from what I was doing, so I never consulted them.

Had Japanese American leaders known of my position while they were still in Seattle, they would have confronted me and said, "You are not even dry behind the ears. How can you take such a step that will create difficulties for the whole group? How do you know there won't be a backlash? How do you know you are right and the rest of us are wrong?" I would have had difficulty answering their questions. But I would have had questions for them also. How could they defend America and the Constitution by acceding to a decision made by military authorities to suspend constitutional guarantees, especially when there had been no suspension of the Constitution via martial law? In the end, I would not have changed their views, and they would not have changed mine. By personality, though, while I had independent positions on various things, I was never what you might call the kind of person who habitually protested.

As I followed the press after the U.S. entered the war, the writing was on the wall. The first part of the evacuation process began with the Bainbridge Islanders, who, because of their proximity to naval installations, were moved in March 1942. The last district in Seattle to be evacuated was the northeast section, including the University District, where I was living. The deadline was May 12, 1942. By the end of March, the Bainbridge Island Japanese Americans were gone. At that point, I knew that I wasn't going. I sat down and wrote a statement:

Why I Refuse to Register for Evacuation

Over and above any man-made creed or law is the natural law of life—the right of human individuals to live and to creatively express themselves. No man was born with the right to limit that law. Nor, do I believe, can anyone justifiably work himself to such a position.

Down through the ages, we have had various individuals doing their bit to establish more securely these fundamental rights. They have tried to help society see the necessity of understanding those fundamental laws; some have succeeded to the extent of having these natural laws recorded. Many have suffered unnatural deaths as a result of their convictions. Yet, today, because of the efforts of some of these individuals, we have recorded in the laws of our nation certain rights for all men and certain additional rights for citizens. These fundamental moral rights and civil liberties are included in the Bill of Rights, U.S. Constitution and other legal records. They guarantee that these fundamental rights shall not be denied without due process of law.

The principles or the ideals are the things which give value to a person's life. They are the qualities which give impetus and purpose toward meaningful experiences. The violation of human personality is the violation of the most sacred thing which man owns.

This order for the mass evacuation of all persons of Japanese descent denies them the right to live. It forces thousands of energetic, law-abiding individuals to exist in a miserable psychological and a horrible physical atmosphere. This order limits to almost the full extent the creative expressions of those subjected. It kills the desire for a higher life. Hope for the future is exterminated. Human personalities are poisoned. The very qualities which are essential to a peaceful, creative community are being thrown out and abused. Over 60 percent are American citizens, yet they are denied on a wholesale scale without due process of law the civil liberties which are theirs.

If I were to register and cooperate under those circumstances, I would be giving helpless consent to the denial of practically all of the things which give me incentive to live. I must maintain my Christian principles. I consider it my duty to maintain the democratic standards for which this nation lives. Therefore, I must refuse this order for evacuation.

Let me add, however, that in refusing to register, I am well aware of the excellent qualities of the army and government personnel connected with the prosecution of this exclusion order. They are men of the finest type, and I sincerely appreciate their sympathetic and honest efforts. Nor do I intend to cast any shadow upon the Japanese and the other Nisei who have registered for evacuation. They have faced tragedy admirably. I am objecting to the principle of this order, which denies the rights of human beings, including citizens. [May 13, 1942]

. . . As removal from Seattle drew near, it occurred to me that if I couldn't tolerate curfew, then how could I agree to be evacuated, which is much worse? I had ignored the curfew order, but the exclusion order was different. If I were roaming the streets, sooner or later I'd be accosted and picked up. On May 16, 1942, I made arrangements with Arthur Barnett to meet me in the morning after the last busload of Japanese left, and he'd drive me over to the FBI. We did this and on the duly appointed day met Special Agent Francis Manion. . . .

After conferring with Assistant U.S. Attorney Gerald Shucklin, who advised that I be given a chance to register for evacuation,

Agent Manion drove me directly to the Maryknoll Registration Center, one the Catholic schools used for registration. After a considerable wait, they said, "You're supposed to sign here."

I said, "That looks like the same registration form I saw a few days ago. Has there been any change in it? No? Well, I can't sign it any more than last week."

Manion responded, "If you don't sign, you're violating the law, and you're subject to some punishment."

I retorted, "I can't do it. What you are going to do as a result of my inability to sign, that's for you to determine. I don't make my decisions on the basis of what I think you're going to do."

Manion took me to a military post, Fort Lawton, and gave me another opportunity to sign. I said, "This is the same form, and I can't sign it." Toward the end of the day, they brought me to the King County Jail, Tank 3C.

Captain Michael A. Revisto, adjutant of the Wartime Civil Control Administration in Seattle, came to see me in jail. There were three headquarters on the West Coast in charge of the uprooting of the Japanese. Revisto, ironically, was an Italian American whose alien relatives were also "enemy aliens." He was cordial and wanted me to register. He reminded me of the violations charged against me: being in an excluded area, refusing to register with the authorities, not being in camp. "The Western Defense is ready to drop everything. We'll give you private escort to Puyallup." I learned that Seattle was the only one of the three western headquarters that didn't have a "perfect record."

Trying to be cooperative: "I can't do that. Get some guy to carry me to the car, drive over there, and dump me inside the camp gate."

Revisto: "I can't do that."

I was flabbergasted. "You mean, you could help process all Japanese Americans without any charge except on the grounds of ancestry, and in clear conscience, you can't do this?" Whenever possible, I tried to separate the objectionable issue from the person administering it. I succeeded in making some good friends that way, and it made it easier to maintain my objections to the issue.

Isn't it interesting how one little incident can stop a person so completely? FBI agent Manion had confiscated my briefcase and found my diary. I had begun my diary the first of May, anticipating some new and strange experiences. During the initial discussion, we had this exchange: "You know, there was another restriction you faced. What did you do about that?"

I responded, "What's that?"

He said, "The curfew restriction. It's in your diary. Were you out after 8 p.m. last night?"

I answered, "Yes. Like you and other Americans, so was I."

Manion: "Oh, then you violated the curfew, too. That would be a 'count two' violation."

I said, "Are you turning yourself in for curfew violation, since you did exactly as I did, and we are both Americans?"

Manion: "Ah, but you are of Japanese ancestry."

I argued, "Has the U.S. Constitution been suspended?"

Manion: "No, not to my knowledge."

I added, "Then, how could a general issue an order that violates the Constitution and the rights of citizens regardless of race, religion, national origin, or creed?"

Manion: "You'll have to take that up with the judge!" We both smiled a little.

In his report to the FBI on our initial discussion, Agent Manion wrote: "It is the principle of the Society of Friends that each person should follow the will of God according to his own convictions. . . . He [Gordon Hirabayashi] could not reconcile the will of God, a part of which was expressed in the Bill of Rights and the U.S. Constitution, with the order discriminating against Japanese aliens and American citizens of Japanese ancestry."

15.

CHARLES KIKUCHI

KICKED OUT OF BERKELEY

April 30, 1942, Berkeley

Today is the day that we are going to get kicked out of Berkeley. It certainly is degrading. I am down here in the control station and I have nothing to do so I am jotting down these notes! The Army Lieutenant over there doesn't want any of the photographers to take pictures of these miserable people waiting for the Greyhound bus because he thinks that the American public might get a sympathetic attitude towards them.

I'm supposed to see my family at Tanforan as Jack told me to give the same family number. I wonder how it is going to be living with them as I haven't done this for years and years? I should have gone over to San Francisco and evacuated with them, but I had a last final to take. I understand that we are going to live in the horse stalls. I hope that the Army has the courtesy to remove the manure first.

This morning I went over to the bank to close my account and the bank teller whom I have never seen before solemnly shook my hand and he said, "Goodbye, have a nice time." I wonder if that isn't the attitude of the American people? They don't seem to be bitter against us, and I certainly don't think I am any different from them. That General DeWitt certainly gripes my ass because he has been listening to the Associated Farmers too much.

Oh, oh, there goes a "thing" in slacks and she is taking pictures of that old Issei lady with a baby. She says she is the official photographer, but I think she ought to leave these people alone. The Nisei around here don't seem to be so sad. They look like they are going on a vacation. They are all gathered around the bulletin board to find out the exact date of their departure. "When are you leaving?" they are saying to one another. Some of those old Issei men must have gone on a binge last night because they smell like *sake*.

Mitch just came over to tell us that I was going on the last bus out of Berkeley with him. Oh, how lucky I am! The Red Cross lady just told me that she would send a truck after my baggage and she wants the phone number. I never had a phone in that dump on Haste Street.

I have a queer sensation and it doesn't seem real. There are smiling faces all around me and there are long faces and gloomy faces too. All kinds of Japanese and Caucasian faces around this place. Soon they will be neurotic cases. Wang thinks that he has an empty feeling in his stomach and I told him to go get a hamburger upstairs because the Church people are handing out free food. I guess this is a major catastrophe so I guess we deserve some free concessions.

The Church people around here seem so nice and full of consideration saying, "Can we store your things?" "Do you need clothes?" "Sank you," the Issei smile even now though they are leaving with hearts full of sorrow. But the Nisei around here seem pretty bold and their manners are brazen. They are demanding service. I guess they are taking advantage of their college educations after all. "The Japs are leaving, hurrah, hurrah!" some little kids are yelling down the street but everybody ignores them. Well, I have to go up to the campus and get the results of my last exam and will barely be able to make it back here in time for the last bus. God, what a prospect to look forward to living among all those Japs!

PART II

THE CAMPS

No one, of course, knows how long the war will last. The government first holds Japanese Americans in hometown detention centers, followed by an indeterminate exile in semipermanent camps farther inland. Over a period of nearly four years, families must confront a series of decisions and actions that will forever define and divide the community and provoke some of the more pointed literature of the camp experience.

FAIRGROUNDS AND RACETRACKS

Once President Roosevelt authorizes mass exclusion, the army's Wartime Civil Control Administration (WCCA) commandeers local racetracks, fairgrounds, and cattle halls for the hasty erection of shacks at fifteen assembly centers to serve as temporary housing until more durable barracks can be built. In the last week of April 1942, a Greyhound bus carries Monica Sone with her family from Seattle's Chinatown thirty-five miles south to the Western Washington Fairgrounds, site of the new Puyallup Assembly Center. On their first night there, the reality of "Life in Camp Harmony" sinks in for her as she tries to sleep under the sweep of a prison searchlight. The shacks are organized into blocks and a nightly "Curfew" is enforced by "block heads" whose newfound authority is resented by a teenaged Mitsuye Yamada, who brings newsprint writing tablets to camp in her suitcase and takes notes for her poems while working the midnight shift at the camp hospital. At the

Portland Assembly Center, Issei poets of the *Bara Ginsha* group struggle with "Resolution and Readiness, Confusion and Doubt" over their unsure futures, including the question of whether they will be safer by repatriating to Japan.

At the Santa Anita Racetrack northeast of Los Angeles, Yoshio Abe opens his novel, *The Man of Dual Nationality*, away from the horse stalls, with a couple kissing on "Lover's Lane," and explores the differences between what's called a "pure" Nisei and a Kibei Nisei, a citizen born in the United States who is sent by his parents to be educated in Japan and returns to America before the war.

DESERTS AND SWAMPS

To carry out the long-term incarceration, the president creates the War Relocation Authority (WRA) as an independent agency that initially reports directly to him. His first director, agricultural official Milton Eisenhower, admits he knows nothing about Japanese Americans and asks the JACL's Mike Masaoka for ideas on how to run the camps. Masaoka provides eighteen pages of recommendations for policies to operate them as indoctrination centers for assimilation and postwar acceptance, with an emphasis on suppression of the Japanese language. Uneasy with his new task as the keeper of concentration camps, Eisenhower complains of having lost a year's sleep in ninety days, and passes the job on to fellow agricultural official Dillon Myer.

By the summer, the army has ten War Relocation Centers ready for occupancy and puts the incarcerees on trains for high deserts and muggy swamps farther inland. Many are sited on the ancestral lands of Indigenous peoples, as ten-year-old Lily Nakai discovers upon her arrival at Amache, Colorado, where Native women board their train to sell them "Fry Bread."

The new arrivals encounter the austere built environment and the harsh physical landscape of their final destinations. In the dust bowl that is Topaz, Utah, Toyo Suyemoto composes a sonnet to capture the first dismal view of her new "Barracks Home." The outrage at finding the camps surrounded by barbed wire, installed in some cases after their arrival, finds expression in "That Damned Fence," a poem that is passed from camp to camp like an underground samizdat, retyped numerous times with textual variants and several different names attached, including one version signed by Supreme Court plaintiff Minoru Yasui and another signed "The Mad Mongolian," Yasui's pen name. One account has the poem surfacing unsigned at Poston, Arizona, during a November 1942 labor strike, posted on bulletin boards and read in the fire circles fueled by oil drums, as depicted on the cover of this book in a painting by imprisoned Disney animator Gene Sogioka. "That Damned Fence" expresses a raw anger that would not have been permitted in the incarceree newspapers, magazines, and literary journals that begin to be published in the camps under the eye of WRA censors. Pressed by the tens of thousands into a confined space with little privacy, people eventually fall into daily routines: eating in the mess hall, taking communal showers, making art. At Poston, Kiyo Sato finds a job as a nursery-school attendant while always aware that "I Am a Prisoner in a Concentration Camp in My Own Country." At Gila River, Masae Wada celebrates the irrigation of the arid Arizona desert with her "Gila Relocation Center Song," with lyrics set to the tune of the school song of Waseda University in Tokyo. But by the first anniversary of their imprisonment, *Minidoka Irrigator* co-editor Cherry Tanaka can take no more and tests the limits of censorship of her Feminidoka column in "The Unpleasantness of the Year."

A more tragic outcome of social pressure in the mess halls and barracks is the ostracism of a fictional young woman who flees Poston, pregnant from a rape, in "Alice Hasn't Come Home" from Hiroshi Nakamura's *Treadmill*, the only novel known to be written in English by an incarceree while in camp. At Manzanar in California, a revolt against JACL leadership spins out of control as MPs shoot into a crowd and kill two young men, memorialized in a poem by WWI veteran and camp dissenter Joe Kurihara as "The Martyrs of Camp

Manzanar." In "The Paper," journalist Iwao Kawakami also turns to poetry at Topaz to mourn the murder of sixty-three-year-old James Wakasa, who is shot by a guard for walking his dog too close to the fence.

Over time, the Issei arrested after Pearl Harbor are gradually released from federal internment back to their families in the WRA camps. But after eighteen months of separation, Nao Akutsu at Minidoka has exhausted all avenues to free her husband from Fort Missoula and begs Eleanor Roosevelt in a letter handwritten in Japanese to "Send Back the Father of These American Citizens."

REGISTRATION AND SEGREGATION

Only *after* the mass removal do government officials make an effort to determine individual loyalty. Their need is twofold: the War Department wants to reopen the army to Nisei volunteers, and the WRA needs to relocate young men and women from the camps into jobs and colleges in the East and Midwest. But having effectively branded the incarcerees as suspect by their very visible removal and imprisonment, authorities now need a reverse public relations campaign to certify the loyalties and thereby clear the names of individuals for recruitment or relocation. The two agencies in February 1943 launch a second mass registration, a loyalty review program with a twenty-eight-item questionnaire that ends with an oath of allegiance. They combine their questions into one form, alternately titled Statement of United States Citizen of Japanese Ancestry, under the logo of the Selective Service System, or Application for Leave Clearance on the WRA form. For the bureaucracy, it is the perfect paper trail, and officials assume affirmative answers as a matter of course. For the incarcerees, the last two questions feel like a trap.

For draft-age men, answering "yes" to question 27, to say they would be willing to serve in the armed forces of the United States, could mean they have just enlisted. For the Issei denied a path to naturalized U.S. citizenship, answering "yes" to question 28 and forswearing obedience to the Emperor of Japan could be seen as renouncing their status as Japanese nationals and could leave them as stateless persons; for the Nisei, a "yes" could be taken as admitting to having previously harbored such an allegiance to a foreign power, and having that used as evidence against them in some unknown future tribunal. No one, not even the camp administration, knows the consequences of a "yes" or "no" answer. At Topaz, thirty-three members of a Resident Committee quickly adopt a set of conditions for answering the questionnaire, including restoration of their civil rights and the chance to return home, and teletype their statement to the secretary of war and the WRA's Dillon Myer, which ends "We Respectfully Ask for Immediate Answers."

Officials are taken by surprise when one in five Nisei in camp either refuse to answer, qualify their answers, or answer "no" to one of the final two questions. At Tule Lake, California, thirty-five young men in Block 42 sign a statement refusing to register, and the project director sends MPs armed with bayonets and submachine guns to surround their mess hall and arrest them, only to learn that the threat of fines and imprisonment for refusing to answer is legally unenforceable. The show of force infuriates Kentaro Takatsui, a hotel operator and recent Buddhist seminary student, who joins them in solidarity with "The Factual Causes and Reasons Why I Refused to Register." Most in the ten camps, however, do reply with a "yes," a position expressed with flag-waving fervor in "Loyalty" by Sada Murayama, the USO director at Tule Lake. An affirmative answer earns Mitsuye Yamada her release from Minidoka for a job in "Cincinnati," where she finds there is no escaping from wartime hostility.

The binary nature of registration effectively creates an administrative class of people who must be designated on paper as *not* loyal for failing to answer a straight "yes." Congress demands that the WRA separate the "no-no" from the "yes-yes." JACL is already in support of a crackdown, having suffered the beatings of its leaders at Manzanar and Poston. In a confidential statement to WRA director Dillon Myer, Mike

Masaoka equates camp dissent with disloyalty to the government and pledges JACL will identify what he calls "known agitators and troublemakers" for segregation and removal. Myer designates Tule Lake as his segregation center and appoints a new, get-tough project director, Raymond Best, who fortifies the camp with twenty-two more watchtowers, an eight-foot-high, double man-proof fence, and a battalion of military police at the ready. The WRA moves out six thousand from Tule Lake who answer "yes" and moves in twelve thousand from the other nine camps. MPs fingerprint the new arrivals and take their mug shots, prompting the narrator of Kazuo Kawai's novel, *The Age*, to observe "This Is Like Going to Prison." Kawai's story captures the sense of dislocation felt by people who have been forcibly removed to their third camp in eighteen months, and shows how segregation breaks up families, with a son who answers "no" separated from his mother who answers "yes."

Tule Lake quickly erupts into turmoil when officials allow a teenager to drive a truck that flips over and kills a farm worker, triggering a camp-wide labor strike and the election of a Negotiating Committee led by two opponents of registration, the Rev. Shizuo Kai and George Kuratomi. Best brings in strikebreakers from other camps and on November 4, when lookouts spot trucks taking their food under cover of darkness from a warehouse to the strikebreakers, segregees clash with MPs in a melee that the WRA falsely reports to newspapers as a riot. As journalist Noboru Shirai reports, "The Army Takes Control" with MPs arresting and savagely beating several men, then throwing them into a military stockade—a prison within a prison. Three *tanka* by Hyakuissei Okamoto capture the mood after "Several brethren arrested after martial law was declared at Tule Lake in November 1943," while poet Violet Kazue de Cristoforo writes of her "Brother's Imprisonment" in the stockade after his beating and works to free him. Kuratomi eludes capture for a month but surrenders to avoid reprisals against the population and is also sent to the stockade, where he meets Tatsuo Inouye, who records in his stockade diary the resolve of the inmates to go on a "Hunger Strike" for their release. Inouye hides his diary from guards and fellow inmates by tightly rolling each page and pushing them with a chopstick inside the pleats of a corrugated cardboard box he keeps near his army-issue cot.

Three Kibei Nisei fiction writers and poets—Jōji Nozawa, Kazuo Kawai, and Masao Yamashiro—answer the crackdown by founding and editing a high-quality, peer-reviewed literary magazine called *Tessaku*, which translates as "Iron Fence" or even "Iron Stockade." Under the guidance of published Issei poet Bunichi Kagawa, the magazine eschews the imitation of Japanese literature, the praise of natural beauty, and expressions of nostalgia for Japan prevalent in other Issei journals, instead nurturing an authentic camp literature that confronts the reality of their lives in a segregation center without beautiful flowers. Kagawa provides an example for his comrades of how to explore literary themes in things that may appear at first to be trivial, like "*Geta*," wooden clogs that raise their feet above the desert sand and mud. After the publication of each issue, the editors hold a review session to critique each other's work. They publish nine issues with print runs of one thousand mimeographed copies each that are snapped up at the Tule Lake Co-op and at other camps by Issei and Kibei Nisei hungry for novels and stories in Japanese. Kawai's novel appears in *Tessaku*, serialized over six issues, along with the short stories by Tanisaki and Nozawa that appear in this volume.

VOLUNTEERS AND THE DRAFT

One goal of the loyalty questionnaire, the recruitment of volunteers for the army, falls short as only about one thousand men enlist from the camps, a fraction of those eligible for service. The JACL's Masaoka is disappointed that the army asks only for volunteers and does not draft men from camp on an equal basis with others, and that those who do volunteer are racially segregated into an army unit led by white officers, the 442nd Regimental Combat Team, rather than integrated throughout the armed services. At Minidoka,

Minoru Masuda weighs the injustice of incarceration against his desire to serve and makes "A Lonely and Personal Decision" to enlist as a medic. He is among those inducted into the 442nd, which is later joined by the 100th Battalion of former National Guardsmen from Hawai'i for combat in Europe. Volunteers already proficient in some Japanese are recruited as translators for the Military Intelligence Service Language School in Minnesota. At Fort Snelling, aspiring sociologist Tamotsu Shibutani takes notes on raucous conversations among MIS students during the day and sits in the latrine late at night after lights-out to type up and preserve the language he hears in "The Activation of Company K," which is peppered with youthful profanity and slang such as "Boochie" for someone who is Japanese.

The call for volunteers divides the Issei as well as the Nisei. In "She Is My Mother, and I Am the Son Who Volunteered," a chapter from Toshio Mori's novella, *The Brothers Murata*, the mother of a young Nisei at Topaz argues with her disapproving peers in defense of her son's decision to enlist. Jōji Nozawa's story, "Father of Volunteers," published in *Tessaku* and newly translated here, takes us behind the faces of Issei parents who are photographed mutely holding a Gold Star flag for the loss of a son in combat to expose the revulsion of one man upon realizing the exploitation of his suffering.

The War Department is so pleased with the performance of its Nisei volunteers that it finally accepts JACL's call to restore military conscription for all Nisei men in camp. At Minidoka, the mothers of draft-age men argue that their sons will be dying for nothing if they are sent to the front without first having their rights as citizens restored. Journalist Fuyo Tanagi leads the writing of a "Petition to President Roosevelt" to which 101 Issei women sign on as the Mothers Society of Minidoka. At Heart Mountain, Yoshito Kuromiya stands at a mass meeting of the "Fair Play Committee" to declare his intention to resist the draft as a test case challenging the underlying unconstitutionality of the camps themselves.

Using a borrowed typewriter in the barracks he shares with his wife and children, grocer Frank Emi laboriously types the

FPC's manifesto onto a mimeograph stencil, underlining the pivotal words that cross the line from protest to resistance, declaring "We Hereby Refuse" to report for induction until their constitutional rights are first restored and their families released from camp. It is the largest organized camp resistance, and the Justice Department indicts sixty-three young men from Heart Mountain for draft evasion in the largest mass trial for draft resistance in U.S. history. Awaiting trial in the Cheyenne County Jail, Eddie Yanagisako and Kenroku Sumida keep spirits high by composing a jailhouse "Song of Cheyenne" their guards cannot understand, sung to the tune of the Holehole bushi, a Hawaiian plantation work song. We found the lyrics on a worn scrap of paper that was carried for fifty years by one of the resisters in his wallet.

RESEGREGATION AND RENUNCIATION

The stereotype of the Tule Lake Segregation Center that persists to this day is that of a pro-Japan population fanatically disloyal to America. What the literature reveals is a people rejected by their country and stripped of everything but their own skin, their own race and culture. Prisonlike conditions feed the formation of prison gangs that call for a resegregation—the separation of those urging the study of Japanese language and literature from the fence-sitters who only wish to be left alone for the duration.

At the same time, lawmakers in Congress seek a means of stripping the Nisei of their citizenship and deporting both Issei and Nisei to Japan, a demand intensified by the perceived failure of the loyalty registration. To get around the constitutional guarantee of birthright citizenship, the attorney general suggests a workaround: give the Nisei the chance to *voluntarily* renounce their citizenship during times of war.

Congressional passage of the Denaturalization Act in July of 1944 sets the trap and fuels radicalization at the segregation center. In "*Wa Shoi Wa Shoi*, the Emergence of the 'Headband' Group," Noboru Shirai examines the single most misunderstood and maligned consequence of the incarceration experience: the *Hokoku Hoshi-dan*, or Volunteers for the Immediate Return to the Homeland, which rallies the people to train themselves for a new life in Japan—not the real nation devastated by war, but a phantom, idealized promised land where they believe they will be treated with dignity once again. Motomu Akashi provides a rare insider's account of teenagers like himself who wear the *hachimaki* headbands and rising-sun sweatshirts and blow their bugles as "Badges of Honor." He shows their threatening-looking marches to be little more than prison calisthenics, and their fervor for the emperor and the study of the Japanese language to be acts of cultural affinity more than political loyalty—personal pride in the only thing the government has left them: "For the first time, I felt good about being Japanese, not in a political or loyalty sense but being part of the Japanese race."

Under the duress of incarceration and segregation, with only rumor and misinformation to guide them, renunciation of their American citizenship becomes the last act of defiance for fifty-five hundred incarcerees, mostly at Tule Lake, who sign papers to repatriate—or expatriate in the case of American-born Nisei who have never known Japan. Joe Kurihara, the U.S. Army veteran of WWI, embraces his expatriation as the culmination of years of enduring racism and hatred with his contemptuous "Japs They Are, Citizens or Not." Others immediately regret their renunciation and petition to withdraw it, as does Hiroshi Kashiwagi in "Starting from Loomis . . . Again." Kashiwagi will spend the next ten years fighting to get back his U.S. citizenship. With the end of the war, his family is among the last to leave Tule Lake, itself the last of the WRA camps to close in March 1946. Like inmates released from prison, the few hundred remaining with nowhere to go are given twenty-five dollars and put on a train for a family detention camp in Crystal City, Texas.

Fairgrounds and Racetracks

16.

MONICA SONE

LIFE IN CAMP HARMONY

As we coasted down Beacon Hill bridge for the last time, we fell silent, and stared out at the delicately flushed morning sky of Puget Sound. We drove through bustling Chinatown, and in a few minutes arrived on the corner of Eighth and Lane. This area was ordinarily lonely and deserted but now it was gradually filling up with silent, labeled Japanese, standing self-consciously among their seabags and suitcases.

Everyone was dressed casually, each according to his idea of where he would be going. One Issei was wearing a thick mackinaw jacket and cleated, high-topped hiking boots. I stared admiringly at one handsome couple, standing slim and poised in their ski clothes. They looked newly wed. They stood holding hands beside their streamlined luggage that matched smartly with the new Mr. and Mrs. look. With an air of resigned sacrifice, some Issei women wore dark-colored slacks with deep-hemmed cuffs. One gnarled old grandmother wore an ankle-length black crepe dress with a plastic initial "S" pinned to its high neckline. It was old-fashioned, but dignified and womanly.

Automobiles rolled up to the curb, one after another, discharging more Japanese and more baggage. Finally at ten o'clock, a vanguard of Greyhound busses purred in and parked themselves neatly along the curb. The crowd stirred and murmured. The bus doors opened and from each, a soldier with rifle in hand stepped out and stood stiffly at attention by the door. The murmuring died. It was the first time I had seen a rifle at such close range and I felt uncomfortable. This rifle was presumably to quell riots, but contrarily, I felt riotous emotion mounting in my breast.

Jim Shigeno, one of the leaders of the Japanese American Citizens League, stepped briskly up front and started reading off family numbers to fill the first bus. Our number came up and we pushed our way out of the crowd. Jim said, "Step right in." We bumped into each other in nervous haste. I glanced nervously at the soldier and his rifle, and I was startled to see that he was but a young man, pink-cheeked, his clear gray eyes staring impassively ahead. I felt that the occasion probably held for him a sort of tense anxiety as it did for us. Henry found a seat by a window and hung out, watching for Minnie who had promised to see him off. Sumi and I suddenly turned maternal and hovered over Mother and Father to see that they were comfortably settled. They were silent.

Newspaper photographers with flash-bulb cameras pushed busily through the crowd. One of them rushed up to our bus, and asked a young couple and their little boy to step out and stand by the door for a shot. They were reluctant, but the photographers were persistent and at length they got out of the bus and posed, grinning widely to cover their embarrassment. We saw the picture in the newspaper shortly after and the caption underneath it read, "Japs good-natured about evacuation."

Our bus quickly filled to capacity. All eyes were fixed up front, waiting. The guard stepped inside, sat by the door, and nodded curtly to the gray-uniformed bus driver. The door closed with a low hiss. We were now the Wartime Civil Control Administration's babies.

When all the busses were filled with the first contingent of Japanese, they started creeping forward slowly. We looked out of the window, smiled and feebly waved our hands at the crowd of friends who would be following us within the next two days. From among the Japanese faces, I picked out the tall, spare figures of our young people's minister, the Reverend

Everett Thompson, and the Reverend Emery Andrews of the Japanese Baptist Church. They were old friends, having been with us for many years. They wore bright smiles on their faces and waved vigorously as if to lift our morale. But Miss Mahon, the principal of our Bailey Gatzert Grammar School and a much-beloved figure in our community, stood in front of the quiet crowd of Japanese and wept openly.

Sumi suddenly spied Minnie, driving her family car. The car screeched to a halt and Minnie leaped out, looking frantically for Henry. Henry flung his window up and shouted, "Minnie! Minnie! Over here!" The bystanders, suddenly good-humored, directed her to our moving bus. Minnie ran up to the windows, puffing, "Sorry I was late, Henry! Here, flowers for you." She thrust a bouquet of fresh yellow daffodils into his outstretched hand. Henry shouted, "Thanks—be seeing you, I hope."

When our bus turned a corner and we no longer had to smile and wave, we settled back gravely in our seats. Everyone was quiet except for a chattering group of university students who soon started singing college songs. A few people turned and glared at them, which only served to increase the volume of their singing. Then suddenly a baby's sharp cry rose indignantly above the hubbub. The singing stopped immediately, followed by a guilty silence. Three seats behind us, a young mother held a wailing red-faced infant in her arms, bouncing it up and down. Its angry little face emerged from multiple layers of kimonos, sweaters and blankets, and it, too, wore the white pasteboard tag pinned to its blanket. A young man stammered out an apology as the mother gave him a wrathful look. She hunted frantically for a bottle of milk in a shopping bag, and we all relaxed when she had found it.

We sped out of the city southward along beautiful stretches of farmland, with dark, newly turned soil. In the beginning we devoured every bit of scenery which flashed past our window and admired the massive-muscled work horses plodding along the edge of the highway, the rich burnished copper color of a browsing herd of cattle, the vivid spring green of the pastures, but eventually the sameness of the country landscape palled on us. We tried to sleep to escape from the restless anxiety which kept bobbing up to the surface of our minds. I awoke with a start when the bus filled with excited buzzing. A small group of straw-hatted Japanese farmers stood by the highway, waving at us. I felt a sudden warmth toward them, then a twinge of pity. They would be joining us soon.

About noon we crept into a small town. Someone said, "Looks like Puyallup, all right." Parents of small children babbled excitedly, "Stand up quickly and look over there. See all the chick-chicks and fat little piggies?" One little city boy stared hard at the hogs and said tersely, "They're *bachi*— dirty!"

Our bus idled a moment at the traffic signal and we noticed at the left of us an entire block filled with neat rows of low shacks, resembling chicken houses. Someone commented on it with awe, "Just look at those chicken houses. They sure go in for poultry in a big way here." Slowly the bus made a left turn, drove through a wire-fenced gate, and to our dismay, we were inside the oversized chicken farm. The bus driver opened the door, the guard stepped out and stationed himself at the door again. Jim, the young man who had shepherded us into the busses, popped his head inside and sang out, "Okay, folks, all off at Yokohama, Puyallup."

We stumbled out, stunned, dragging our bundles after us. It must have rained hard the night before in Puyallup, for we sank ankle deep into gray, glutinous mud. The receptionist, a white man, instructed us courteously, "Now, folks, please stay together as family units and line up. You'll be assigned your apartment."

We were standing in Area A, the mammoth parking lot of the state fairgrounds. There were three other separate areas, B, C and D, all built on the fairgrounds proper, near the baseball field and the race tracks. This camp of army barracks was hopefully called Camp Harmony.

We were assigned to apartment 2–I–A, right across from the bachelor quarters. The apartments resembled elongated, low stables about two blocks long. Our home was one room, about 18 by 20 feet, the size of a living room. There was one small window in the wall opposite the one door. It was bare except for a small, tinny wood-burning stove crouching in the center. The flooring consisted of two by fours laid directly on the earth, and dandelions were already pushing their way up through the cracks, Mother was delighted when she saw their shaggy yellow heads. "Don't anyone pick them. I'm going to cultivate them."

Father snorted, "Cultivate them! If we don't watch out, those things will be growing out of our hair."

Just then Henry stomped inside, bringing the rest of our baggage. "What's all the excitement about?"

Sumi replied laconically, "Dandelions."

Henry tore off a fistful. Mother scolded, "*Arra! Arra!* Stop that. They're the only beautiful things around here. We could have a garden right in here."

"Are you joking, Mama?"

I chided Henry, "Of course, she's not. After all, she has to have some inspiration to write poems, you know, with all the *'nali keli's.'* I can think of a poem myself right now:

> Oh, Dandelion, Dandelion,
> Despised and uprooted by all,
> Dance and bob your golden heads
> For you've finally found your home
> With your yellow fellows, *nali keli*, amen!"

Henry said, thrusting the dandelions in Mother's black hair, "I think you can do ten times better than that, Mama."

Sumi reclined on her seabag and fretted, "Where do we sleep? Not on the floor, I hope."

"Stop worrying," Henry replied disgustedly.

Mother and Father wandered out to see what the other folks were doing and they found people wandering in the mud, wondering what other folks were doing. Mother returned shortly, her face lit up in an ecstatic smile, "We're in luck. The latrine is right nearby. We won't have to walk blocks."

We laughed, marveling at Mother who could be so poetic and yet so practical. Father came back, bent double like a woodcutter in a fairy tale, with stacks of scrap lumber over his shoulder. His coat and trouser pockets bulged with nails. Father dumped his loot in a corner and explained, "There was a pile of wood left by the carpenters and hundreds of nails scattered loose. Everybody was picking them up, and I hustled right in with them. Now maybe we can live in style with tables and chairs."

The block leader knocked at our door and announced lunchtime. He instructed us to take our meal at the nearest mess hall. As I untied my seabag to get out my pie plate, tin cup, spoon and fork, I realized I was hungry. At the mess hall we found a long line of people. Children darted in and out of the line, skiing in the slithery mud. The young stood impatiently on one foot, then the other, and scowled, "The food had better be good after all this wait." But the Issei stood quietly, arms folded, saying very little. A light drizzle began to fall, coating bare black heads with tiny sparkling raindrops. The chow line inched forward.

Lunch consisted of two canned sausages, one lob of boiled potato, and a slab of bread. Our family had to split up, for the hall was too crowded for us to sit together. I wandered up and down the aisles, back and forth along the crowded tables and benches, looking for a few inches to squeeze into. A small Issei woman finished her meal, stood up and hoisted her legs modestly over the bench, leaving a space for one. Even as I thrust myself into the breach, the space had shrunk to two inches, but I worked myself into it. My dinner companion, hooked just inside my right elbow, was a bald headed, gruff-looking Issei man who seemed to resent nestling at mealtime. Under my left elbow was a tiny, mud-spattered girl. With busy runny nose, she was belaboring her sausages, tearing them into shreds and mixing them into the potato gruel which she had made with water. I choked my food down.

We cheered loudly when trucks rolled by, distributing canvas army cots for the young and hardy, and steel cots for the older folks. Henry directed the arrangement of the cots. Father and Mother were to occupy the corner nearest the wood stove. In the other corner, Henry arranged two cots in L shape and announced that this was the combination living room–bedroom area, to be occupied by Sumi and myself. He fixed a male den for himself in the corner nearest the door. If I had had my way, I would have arranged everyone's cots in one neat row as in Father's hotel dormitory.

We felt fortunate to be assigned to a room at the end of the barracks because we had just one neighbor to worry about. The partition wall separating the rooms was only seven feet high with an opening of four feet at the top, so at night, Mrs. Funai next door could tell when Sumi was still sitting up in bed in the dark, putting her hair up. "*Mah*, Sumi-chan," Mrs. Funai would say through the plank wall, "are you curling your hair tonight again? Do you put it up every night?" Sumi would put her hands on her hips and glare defiantly at the wall.

The block monitor, an impressive Nisei who looked like a star tackle with his crouching walk, came around the first night to tell us that we must all be inside our room by nine o'clock every night. At ten o'clock, he rapped at the door again, yelling, "Lights out!" and Mother rushed to turn the light off not a second later.

Throughout the barracks, there were a medley of creaking cots, whimpering infants and explosive night coughs. Our attention was riveted on the intense little wood stove which glowed so violently I feared it would melt right down to the floor. We soon learned that this condition lasted for only a short time, after which it suddenly turned into a deep freeze. Henry and Father took turns at the stove to produce the harrowing blast which all but singed our army blankets, but did not penetrate through them. As it grew quieter in the barracks, I could hear the light patter of rain. Soon I felt the "splat! splat!" of raindrops digging holes into my face. The dampness on my pillow spread like a mortal bleeding, and I finally had to get out and haul my cot toward the center of the room. In a short while Henry was up. "I've got multiple leaks, too. Have to complain to the landlord first thing in the morning."

All through the night I heard people getting up, dragging cots around. I stared at our little window, unable to sleep. I was glad Mother had put up a makeshift curtain on the window for I noticed a powerful beam of light sweeping across it every few seconds. The lights came from high towers placed around the camp where guards with Tommy guns kept a twenty-four-hour vigil. I remembered the wire fence encircling us, and a knot of anger tightened in my breast. What was I doing behind a fence like a criminal? If there were accusations to be made, why hadn't I been given a fair trial? Maybe I wasn't considered an American anymore. My citizenship wasn't real, after all. Then what was I? I was certainly not a citizen of Japan as my parents were. On second thought, even Father and Mother were more alien residents of the United States than Japanese nationals for they had little tie with their mother country. In their twenty-five years in America, they had worked and paid their taxes to their adopted government as any other citizen.

Of one thing I was sure. The wire fence was real. I no longer had the right to walk out of it. It was because I had Japanese ancestors. It was also because some people had little faith in the ideas and ideals of democracy. They said that after all these were but words and could not possibly insure loyalty. New laws and camps were surer devices. I finally buried my face in my pillow to wipe out burning thoughts and snatch what sleep I could.

17.

MITSUYE YAMADA

CURFEW

In our area
was a block head
who told us
what's what
in a warden's helmet.

Turn off your lights
it's curfew time!

I was reading
with a flashlight
under my blanket
but the barracks boards
in the hot sun
had shrunk slyly
telling
bars of light

Off with your lights.

There must be no light.

18

PORTLAND SENRYŪ POETS

RESOLUTION AND READINESS, CONFUSION AND DOUBT

*Translated by Shelley Baker-Gard,
Michael Freiling, and Satsuki Takikawa*

BY JŌNAN

juu man ga kakugo shite ita ima no ichi

for these current times
all 100,000 of us
made ready

BY MOKUGYO

sore to naku chichi wa yuigon jyou wo kaki

whatever is next—
father has already written
his final wishes

BY JŌNAN

ubugoe wo matsuma haha-oya ochitsukazu

our mother too
awaits the baby's first cry
all on edge

BY GOICHI

idou chi mo kiwamari wakareru hi ga semari

decided now
my new destination—
our breakup is near

BY JŌNAN

wakimaete ita ni kishaba de 'horori' suru

at the train station
my self-control departs
and tears arrive

BY ROSHYOU

eijuu mo kikoku mo tsukazu hi ga sugiru

stay forever or return home
the decision never made—
just too much to bear

BY SEN TARO

utagai no aru nashi to wazu shuuyoushi

they never asked
suspicious or not—
just put us away

19

YOSHIO ABE

LOVER'S LANE

Translated by Fumio Takamae

"I don't feel sad, nor do I hear music," she said, shrugging her shoulders as she removed her lips from his. The shoulders supporting her thickly bobbed hair seemed thin and frail, more suitable to a girl sitting on the spacious lawn of a high school campus. Yet, here she was already nineteen, and the setting was roadside grass framed by shrubbery.

She shook her dark hair and looked a bit affected. As her hair moved over her face, she stuck out her tongue which she had not pushed into his mouth when they had kissed.

"All I felt was a tickle," she said. She seemed to be amusing herself by sticking out her tongue, and not letting him see it. She stared at the stubble around his mouth which finally seemed to be taking the form of a beard and mustache. The quick pain caused by that stubble had disappeared, and she now felt a pleasant sensation, perhaps as intense as that of onion springs brushing the back of her calves. Hardly the rapture she had expected from a kiss.

"Say something, Tak. Or should I call you Takeshi, now that you're Japanese again?"

When she next jerked her head, Takeshi Iwamura took his arm from her back and leaned back with both hands on the grass, his legs sprawled alongside hers. Directly ahead there was a low fence of semi-circular design made with bamboo splits imported from Japan. Beyond the fence stretched a gravel lane, and beyond that there was more shrubbery and a chain link fence. The fence seemed never to end, and on its top ran strands of barbed wire. The fence posts bent inward, faintly suggesting boomerangs. Takeshi looked past the fence and beyond the barbed wire. His gaze was that of a caged man, fixed on that space beyond. It brimmed with hate and scorn as he experienced once more that strangely mixed sensation of feeling both trapped and secure.

The evening sun in Southern California, which casts no shadows, had set long ago, resembling a sunflower being dipped into a thin reddish clay. Now came the long twilight which would slowly turn into night. Dusk in Southern California always seemed vague with no clear boundary between day and night, almost like its indistinct seasons. The horizon was also undefined. Where did the land end? The houses with their eucalyptus and their groves of olive and orange trees seemed afloat, with asphalt roads now yellowing and changing into canals. The sky kept its color, as if it were a silver-gray parachute below which we all dangled. Only where there were patches of mist, or races of smog resembling a faded dress on a clothesline, could one make out a horizon. Iwamura felt no attachment to this strange scenery. He felt only anger at being separate from the community located in that very scenery. Yet, mixed with the anger was the absurdity of not being able to walk freely toward it.

"Takeshi, are you alive?"

She had pinched his cheek in asking the question, and the arms supporting his body relaxed.

"You said I'm Japanese again, didn't you? Do you think being Japanese means being put in a cage with a group of Japanese and Nisei? We're neither Americans nor Japanese; we're Indians. I don't care what you call me, Takeshi or Tak. Any name is better than a number, now that we're listed by numbers. If you now fancy yourself a Japanese, do I call you Sumiko and not Sue?"

"No . . ."

Since she had discovered that the name Sumiko contained the word *sumi*, the Japanese word for India ink, she had not permitted even her parents to call her Sumiko. Even after she had been told that *sumi* also meant purity, she had stubbornly insisted on being called Sue.

"One minute you're quiet, then you open your mouth and words emerge like a chain of sausages," she said.

"As for my sausage," he interrupted. . . .

"That's a filthy association. You're forgetting that I'm a lady."

"I too feel no sorrow and hear no music, and it's too bad you can't understand that. I've this feeling of having been betrayed. The military came, took my body and left the rest behind. There can't be any real feeling of sadness."

"But you are, after all, Kibei. It's in the way you quibble. You're like the Issei, but younger. You're as pathetic as Tchaikowsky's Sixth."

She turned, after her retort, and looked directly at him. His face was emotionless, as if it were without life. About a week before, she had told him of her thought that he must have been born in Hawaii, even though he was a Kibei. It had not been meant as criticism. Yet, he refused the comment. Issei and Nisei, one born in Japan, the other in America. This generational distinction, he understood and accepted. But he could not accept the distinction between Kibei and Nisei. After all, Kibei was a Nisei who had been sent to Japan for educational purposes and then had returned. Why were they separate from the so-called "pure" Nisei? Iwamura shut his eyes and mouth tightly at Sue's reminder that he was a Kibei.

She began to giggle. There were still traces of lipstick around his mouth. She had intended only to brush his lips with hers. His mouth now both attracted and repelled her, in part because of her inexperience. She wanted to continue teasing him . . .

"Don't move. I'm going to remove the lipstick traces."

She took a small handkerchief from her blouse sleeve. She'd been told by a music teacher that a handkerchief could be kept in the sleeve, somewhat like a sweatpad. That same teacher would see that her high school diploma was sent to her, now that she could not attend commencement.

Iwamura opened his eyes, watching Sue as she wiped his mouth. The handkerchief seemed odorless, but her perfume stirred him. His first impulse was to say cynically, at least it doesn't smell of horses, but he swallowed the remark quickly. A few years earlier when he had just come back from Japan, he would have said aloud whatever he was thinking. He knew that American women, especially Nisei, were somewhat sensitive about the smell of their hair and their body, especially if it suggested anything animal. Sue now lived in a converted horse stable, not in the barracks, and she used, therefore, more perfume than she really needed, feeling always that nothing would get rid of the smell of horses. The stable had been sterilized with lime, and army cots had been brought in. It resembled an army camp. Compared to these accommodations, the barracks which had been built on what was once the parking lot, seemed more fit for humans, even though they resembled locker rooms built on the seashore. Those living in the converted stables were called "grooms" by those inhabiting the barracks. The grooms' usual retort was that though we live in stalls, we have at least an exclusive area lined with willow trees, while you barrack dwellers live in outhouses in the desert. You're like nightcrawlers or ants confined to a waffle iron. These abusive exchanges started with crinkled noses, but ended quickly in hollow grins when the realization struck both groups that they were Japanese and confined. . . .

Her face was so close, like a lighted bed lamp. Her hair which merged with the dark of the night sky seemed far away. The freckles under her eyes made her youthful freshness disappear and now gave her face an inexplicably tired look. Long before tapping his teeth as if they were piano keys, she had been a playful high school senior. Now, suddenly, she became a woman with the melancholy look of a prostitute drinking a glass of wine in the corner of a bar. Had she had a man before? It didn't matter whether or not she had been a virgin. This face had been robbed of things more important than virginity: her home, her puppy that had been taken away, her father who had been sent to the detention camp in Montana. Here she was in a stable with her mother and brother. She had also been robbed of her piano. We are virtually deprived of the American citizenship which the Issei wanted their Nisei children to have so that they could safely live in the United States. She had also been robbed of her American citizenship. Hers was the face of someone who had been ransacked, a mask hiding all that had been taken. Her smile is a pretense which mocks her and mocks me by telling me not to be too serious, thought Iwamura. It doesn't matter whether she's had other men or not, but she should know that she's had things taken from her—yet, what power do I have, since I've been robbed, to give her something for what she has lost. The power of love? Love's impossible when blood is being shed by American and Japanese soldiers; it's impossible when enemy aliens, the loyal Japanese and their offspring, are interned together. Iwamura bit Sue's finger hard. She felt the pain and wondered whether he had bitten through to the bone, but did not pull her finger out. She knew that would hurt even more and cause it to bleed. The pain that she felt in her arm was his pain. Her face lost its tiredness and became youthful again. Her freckles beamed like sunlight through leaves. Her big eyes shone like grapes in the sun.

"You've been hurt. You really have," she whispered, as if the saliva caught in her throat was distorting the sound of her words.

The couple who had been whispering, laughing, skulking and groaning in the shrubbery behind them came out one after the other and went walking down the lane, their arms around each other's waists and shoulders, entangled loosely like puppies playing with each other. This was lover's lane, away from the barracks, the stables, and the grandstand, although the sky was still light, the lane between the shrubbery and the barbed wire took on shadows. A patrol jeep came along outside the barbed wire, with two soldiers, their helmets on. One drove and the other had a rifle under his arm. The jeep slowed, then stopped, and the soldiers peered inside as if they were at a zoo which had just closed. Sensing their presence, Iwamura got up.

"Hubba, hubba, hubba!" The soldiers were looking at Sue, particularly at her legs. The driver made a throaty sound.

"Go to hell, you shit-asses!" Iwamura shouted at them and grabbed at the grass. Had there been stones at hand, he would have thrown them. He wondered suddenly if Sue had panties on since the soldiers kept looking between her legs.

"Hey! Beat it," Iwamura shouted as if he were a butcher driving away dogs. The soldier with the gun looked at Iwamura and ran his finger across his throat, making a slitting sound.

Sue started to laugh after they had gone. She pushed her cheek against his shoulder, all the while laughing. He, too, started to laugh. He felt he understood what caused her to laugh. Although he was angry at her mocking him, he came to the conclusion that she was being somewhat like a monkey in a cage baring its teeth in hostility. Although he found it difficult to excuse what had just happened with the soldiers, he was mature enough to realize that there was no difference between them and those outside the fence, since they were under the same set of military regulations, although perhaps in different positions. Both groups were monkeys on a chain of regulations. Seeing the soldiers drive away, he relaxed.

"They looked like apes in military uniforms, hairy apes." So saying, Sue giggled. Iwamura nodded and grasped her shoulder.

"Well, young lady, would you like to go for an evening's ride? With your scarf flowing in the wind? I used to drive a coupe before I was put here. I sold it. It was a junky old car. Let's go for a ride in that car tonight. I'll have a budding pianist riding beside me. There aren't many cars on the road. We'll go out to the country. See that red signal? It'll turn green just as we get there. Aren't you cold? Let's stop at a drive-in for a bite. Aren't you thirsty? How about a banana split? I'm going to have a can of beer. Don't look at the carhop's legs, did you say? That kerchief apron is too short. Yes, I'm not exactly polite when I'm out with a lady."

"I'd like to go to Santa Monica. I've never ridden on a roller coaster. Take me there."

"Sure. Let's go. See the celery fields? They're all owned by Japanese farmers. At least they used to own them. It's hard work crouching in celery fields. You end up with a stiff back. The same with digging potatoes. The fashionable area of Beverly Hills is way back there. Yeah, I know. The policeman on the motorcycle is just like a highwayman. He gives tickets only to people in junky cars and overlooks speeding violations by those in expensive ones. Light my cigarette with yours, please. Yes, a Chesterfield. It tastes like Japanese cigarettes. The red packs of Lucky Strikes have gone to war—that's their slogan and it's stupid. We're getting near Santa Monica. See there, Ferris wheels, and they look like pearl buttons in the sky. And the roller coaster resembles a railroad with its track in the sky."

Iwamura now began to feel empty at this game of playing "Let's go for a ride," but he continued the game a bit longer. I'm not exactly eager to go on only for the feeling which the game gives me, but at least this isn't a sadness that comes from being deprived of the freedom of pleasure. There is after all something we can't be robbed of. We still have the freedom to imagine. What a pity this is all that's left to us. Who on God's earth has the right to deny Sue or me this freedom?

The night air was turning chilly, and he became aware of Sue's warmth as she walked alongside him, his arm around her shoulders. He likened the lights glittering beyond the barbed wire to the lights of the amusement park on the Santa Monica beach. He thought tenderly of Sue who was immersed in the pleasure of their fantasy; he was fond of her. Since there was a regulation not to sell drivers more than two cans of beer, he could only get partially tipsy in this imaginary game. Sue imagined a banana split and consumed that while he looked at her and thought how adorable she was. She felt that she was making up for the shortage of sugar in the camp by imagining the banana split.

The night wind that rose was chilly, even for May in Southern

California. The two walked along the dark lane toward the stables. There were still other couples on the lane.

They stopped for a while when they reached an opening of sparse willow trees. The trees looked as if they were covered with bandages because the coat of lime which whitened their slender trunks had been worn away in some places. They did not kiss goodbye, feeling that people were watching. Sue only gently touched Iwamura's mouth.

"Your college beard goes better with a pipe, don't you think?" And she called him a college boy. Iwamura grabbed her hand and pressed it with his lips. She quickly pulled her hand away as if from a flame.

"I won't go back to college. I can't. Shit! The damn war! Well, I'm getting serious again. That's it. I really had a good time and I'll sleep with the memory of it. Sue, sweet dreams."

"See you. Good night."

"Good night."

On hearing the wooden cross piece lock shut at the wicket of the stable, Iwamura went out into Seabiscuit Avenue, named after the famous racehorse. On both sides of the avenue leading to the grandstand, and in what used to be a parking lot, there were rows and rows of hastily thrown-up barracks set in an oblong checkerboard pattern. The end of the avenue which seemed so distant in the day time looked surprisingly near in the dark. The searchlight traced its pattern over the rooftops of the barracks, focused on Iwamura, then moved from one side to the other as if to scoop him up. One usually senses danger when the headlights of an oncoming car shine directly and suddenly on a lone figure along the highway. The effect of the searchlight had an even greater impact. Iwamura felt the desperation of a runaway caught by a police searchlight—a desperation enhanced by the helplessness and the knowledge that one was truly innocent. Although he had been caught by the searchlight almost every night for three weeks, he could never get used to it. People said that the beams were turned on women who got up late at night to go to the block toilets. Iwamura now moved closer to the barracks, pretending to look in the windows in an attempt to avoid the searchlights.

One of the camp policemen, a group organized by the detained Japanese, popped out from behind the barracks. He was wearing a helmet which was of little use at night and an armband with C.P. stenciled on it. He saw Iwamura, grinned sheepishly at him, and said, "It's curfew."

Deserts and Swamps

RECOMMENDATIONS TO MILTON EISENHOWER
DIRECTOR, WAR RELOCATION AUTHORITY

April 6, 1942

GENERAL POLICIES:

We believe that all projects should be directed (1) to create "Better Americans In A Greater America"; (2) to maintain a high and healthy morale among the evacuees; (3) to train them to cope with the difficult problems of adjustment and rehabilitation after the war; (4) to permit them to actually and actively participate in the war effort of our nation; and (5) to develop a community spirit of cooperative action and service to others before self. . . .

We suggest that as much intercourse with "white" Americans be permitted as possible. We do not relish the thought of "Little Tokyos" springing up in these resettlement projects, for by so doing we are only perpetuating the very things which we hope to eliminate: those mannerisms and thoughts which mark us apart, aside from our physical characteristics. We hope for a one hundred per cent American community. And, for such a community, it is essential that Caucasian contacts are maintained personally through daily intercourse and not through the medium of letters or books.

DRAFTEE STATUS:

We believe that American citizens of Japanese ancestry should continue to be permitted to serve in the armed forces of the United States. We further hold that the members of the Japanese communities, whether they be in camps or not, should be privileged to participate in any and every government registration or request for service. This is vital for morale.

EDUCATION:

One thing is certain: there should be no Japanese language schools. . . . Special stress should be laid on the enunciation and pronunciation of words so that awkward and "Oriental" sounds will be eliminated. . . .

Respectfully submitted,

/s/ Mike Masaoka

NATIONAL SECRETARY—JACL

20

LILY YURIKO NAKAI HAVEY

FRY BREAD

When did night fall that first day on the train? We traveled hours in the tremulous light that filtered through the shades. Only when I peered out furtively did shafts of light strike me. Then, later, when I peeked, it was dark . . . dark inside, dark outside. I looked around. Most of the people were dozing. A few overhead lights flickered on fitfully as if loathe to awaken. I went back to sleep, cushioning my head with my jacket.

We chugged on and crossed into Arizona on day two.

Somewhere in the middle of this state, the train lurched to a stop, and two dark women heaved themselves onto our coach. We stared at these creased and bronzed apparitions. Their black braids snaked down to their hips. Silver necklaces glinted on their breasts.

"Who are they?" "Look at their clothes." "Get the police," echoed from those sitting around us. Dumbfounded, we sat and stared. Then one of the women smiled, revealing great gaps in her teeth, and boomed, "Nava-jo. You Ha-pa-nee." She dug into a basket slung over her arm and offered squares of something puffy and brown.

"Fry bread," she said.

"That's bread?" I asked. Bread was spongy white, wrapped in waxed paper with colored dots, and had the words "Wonder Bread." These shiny puffs looked like wet cardboard.

"Eat, eat," she urged.

Were they poisoned? Were these women agents sent to kill us? I looked at my mother, but she only shrugged her shoulders. "Smells OK," she said. I hesitated, but hunger won. I nibbled one. It oozed delicious fat.

My mother tasted one. "Ah, *oishii*, delicious," she commented. The women walked through the car, dispensing their bread. "One more? Plenty here."

"Yes, thank you." Both my mother and I accepted seconds.

I savored mine as the women descended into the vast desert and waved us away, arms arcing good-byes, velvet skirts swirling. They were still waving as they dissolved into the gray landscape.

"*Mah, honto ni.* Really." Were they *obake*? Ghosts?

"Where did they come from?"

"Buddha sent them. *Namu amida butsu.*"

When the train pulled away, we fell into bemused wonder. How did they know about us? Did the train really stop? Was this a dream?

I had learned about Navajo Indians in third grade. They were poor, lived in hogans, and kept flocks of sheep. They lived on reservations. Was Amache a reservation? It sounded like one. Were we destined to become another tribe in Colorado? No, the government called it a "relocation center." We were being relocated from California. But why?

We were being sent to a better camp—Mrs. Satomura had explained before we left Santa Anita—farther inland for our own safety; a better, way-better place.

"But I want to go home," I had told her.

"Not until the war is over, Yuriko."

"How long is that?"

"No one knows. Maybe a year."

"That long? Don't you want to go home?"

"We all do. Your mother said you'd visit us when we go back."

"We will."

I had stared so long at the black barracks that Mrs. Satomura had asked, "Are you all right?"

"Santa Anita is a funny home," I had replied.

21

TOYO SUYEMOTO

BARRACKS HOME

This is our barracks, squatting on the ground,
Tar-papered shack, partitioned into rooms
By sheetrock walls, transmitting every sound
Of neighbors' gossip or the sweep of brooms.
The open door welcomes the refugees,
And now at last there is no need to roam
Afar: here space enlarges memories
Beyond the bounds of camp and this new home.

The floor is carpeted with dust, wind-borne
Dry alkali, patterned by insect feet.
What peace can such a place as this impart?
We can but sense, bewildered and forlorn,
That time, disrupted by the war from neat
Routines, must now adjust within the heart.

22.

THAT DAMNED FENCE

They've sunk the posts deep into the ground
They've strung out wires all the way around.
With machine gun nests just over there,
And sentries and soldiers everywhere.

We're trapped like rats in a wired cage,
To fret and fume with impotent rage;
Yonder whispers the lure of the night,
But that DAMNED FENCE assails our sight.

We seek the softness of the midnight air,
But that DAMNED FENCE in the floodlight glare
Awakens unrest in our nocturnal quest,
And mockingly laughs with vicious jest.

With nowhere to go and nothing to do,
We feel terrible, lonesome, and blue:
That DAMNED FENCE is driving us crazy,
Destroying our youth and making us lazy.

Imprisoned in here for a long, long time,
We know we're punished—though we've committed no crime,
Our thoughts are gloomy and enthusiasm damp,
To be locked up in a concentration camp.

Loyalty we know, and patriotism we feel,
To sacrifice our utmost was our ideal,
To fight for our country, and die, perhaps;
But we're here because we happen to be Japs.

We all love life, and our country best,
Our misfortune to be here in the west,
To keep us penned behind that DAMNED FENCE,
Is someone's notion of NATIONAL DEFENCE!

23

KIYO SATO

I AM A PRISONER IN A CONCENTRATION CAMP IN MY OWN COUNTRY

Our camp, they tell us, is now to be called a "relocation center" and not a "concentration camp." We are internees, not prisoners. So now we are "relocated" into a relocation center!

I live in an apartment in a relocation center. I am fed three meals a day. If I don't want to I don't have to work. I am an internee.

Here's the truth: I am now called a non-alien, stripped of my constitutional rights. I am a prisoner in a concentration camp in my own country. I sleep on a canvas cot under which is a suitcase with my life's belongings: a change of clothes, underwear, a notebook and pencil.

Why?

* * *

I am elated, not only to have a job but to have some spending money. Now I can order burlap from Sears & Roebuck for our windows. I'd like to have something bright. Green? Blue? The problem with colored burlap is that it fades in no time where the sun hits. Maybe with my second paycheck I will have enough to replace my army blanket partition with burlap.

First things first: we need some toothbrushes. Mama cleans her teeth with a washcloth wrapped around her finger. And I've got to get some monthly needs. Mama showed me how to fold a piece of a diaper and pin one inside my underwear. I don't like having to change behind my blanket partition, which Tochan hung from the rafters for my privacy. I never know who's going to come looking for me, like my little brother, for instance.

I miss my room where I can read and write and watch the moonlight through my window and hear the symphony of frogs down by the creek. Right now I hear the Sueokas on the other side of the thin wall, and more garbled sounds from three and four walls down. The only privacy I have is inside my small suitcase under my cot.

Here, I shower with a half a dozen people, eat with two hundred and fifty people, and sit in the community latrine with people I don't even know.

To wash out my monthly personals without being noticed, I wrap the soiled diaper squares with my clothes and take them to the laundry room and wait in line with mothers shuffling huge bags of dirty clothes wrapped furoshiki-style with sheets. I carefully unwrap my blouse in the bottom of the deep tub and do my washing. Everything dries up in no time, even inside our rooms, so two sets is all I need. Within an hour I fold the diaper squares and put them inside my suitcase under my cot.

Everybody knows everything about everybody—when you go to the latrine, when you go to the shower room, and on and on. But hardly anyone pays any attention to what one wears. We all came with what we could carry and that's what we wash and wear and mend. The laundry room is never empty. We look so fresh and clean in the mornings, but by mid-afternoon the desert dirt permeates our clothes and body.

Mama mends constantly. No matter when I come in, she is sitting on her cot with her needle and thread. No doubt she wishes she had her old Singer sewing machine. With only a change or two of clothing for each of her eight children, the washing and the mending pursue Mama.

Occasionally I see her take out the few yards of bright green corduroy she brought with her.

"What are you doing with that, Mama?" I ask.

"I think this might fit Tomoko. Maybe a skirt and a vest."

* * *

I live in Block 229, Apartment 11-B in the Poston Relocation Center in Poston, Arizona. With such an address, who can tell that my order from Montgomery Ward is being delivered to prisoner #21716-C? My father is #21716-A and Mama is #21716-B. I am C and down the line to Masashi, who is #21716-K. The government reclassified my brothers and sisters and me from "citizen" to "non-alien," whatever that means.

Soon, with my first month's paycheck of twelve dollars, I plan to decorate our "apartment" windows.

24.

MASAE WADA

GILA RELOCATION CENTER SONG

Translated by Minako Waseda

Waves rolling over the Pacific Ocean
We came over to Gila far away from home
Giant cactus stand dauntless
The deep green everlasting
With this spirit, with these aspirations
Live boldly with ambition
Praise the fortitude, praise the fortitude
Praise, praise the fortitude.

Looking up to the sky, tonight is clear too
A serene mind in the plains of Gila
The stars twinkling across the sky
Distant on our path shines the light of hope
Enduring hardships, we should live
Until the bell of peace finally rings
Look to hope, look to hope
Look to, look to hope.

The floating mirage, the symbol of the ideal
If we cultivate with high spirits
An abundant crop shall fill all the fields
Rouse yourself fellows, proceed resolutely
And thus build the land of our ideals
Reclaim the wasteland, reclaim the wasteland
Reclaim, reclaim the wasteland.

25

CHERRY TANAKA

THE UNPLEASANTNESS
OF THE YEAR

AS INEVITABLY as upon concluding a good magazine novel, my hand turns back the pages to glance once again with different perspective upon the illustration of the story. I turn back in retrospect upon the conclusion of a year in Minidoka to survey the memory-painted pictures there with different eyes from those that first gazed dejectedly over the dusty rows of barracks implanted among the sagebrush that September of last year.

BUT AS IT SIT before my typewriter and conjure up the past with intent reminiscing over the pleasant memories that a year at Hunt brings, I find I cannot write the banal sentimentalities usually associated with a-year-has-gone-by column. In a sudden perverse and pessimistic mood, with each reminiscence the focus of my mind seems but to center on the disagreeableness along with the pleasantness.

Were I to continue as I started out at the onset, I would probably recall the scenic and novel train ride that brought us to Hunt—but I seem only to remember that it was dirty, wearying, and comfortless. Those beginning days of life in wide open plains—where breathing meant not clear, fresh air, but a

lungful of eroded dust where one did not ever forget the normal conveniences accepted in the current mode of living, but
since it must be so, put such "luxuries" in the recesses of one's
mind and bore the stench of the outhouses, the inexpediences
of washing, the cramped one-room quarters.

Reminiscences of home life brings with it the encroachment
of privacy, the unavoidable throwing together of remote strangers, so that one wants to cry out against the infringement of
personal freedom—but such emotions remain pent up and dor-
mant in one's own secret inferno of protestation.

THE HOLIDAY SEASONS and its festivities . . . celebrating
the family dinner on long dining hall tables. The impropriety of
the holiday meat being eaten across from former strangers . . .
while the fourth member of the family washes dishes back in
the kitchen, earning his sixteen dollars. Weekly movies glimpsed
through a thimble's space between obstructing heads after hour
long waits in the numbing and freezing wind.

Sloshing to work in gumbo mud, fighting the suction with
each step and tug . . . step and tug. The discommodity of struggling on boots again to go to the wash room for the comfort of
brushing one's teeth.

Attending church, and shutting one's eyes to the naked rafters overhead, the dust swirling in through cracks, hands rubbing one another to keep warmth circulating, shutting one's
ears to the discordant piano . . . as the sermon is given.

Taking an evening stroll, to find the obstruction of barbed
wires—symbolic in meaning.

NOT A PRETTY PICTURE the memorable scenes of the
past year. Painted rather starkly perhaps, but it is grim reality.
The year of life behind wires was necessitated by war . . . and
war brings not pretty things—war is grim—grim reality.

The unpleasantness of the year will not be the stones laid for
a path to embitterment, but only serves to lend value to the
things one has taken too much for granted . . . the little things
of daily living—the essential conveniences, the seclusion and
security of home and a family group, the appeal of home
cooking, the enjoyment of having a good time, the beauty of a

tree, green foliage, and lawns; and the bigger things—the glory of freedom, the pricelessness of one's rights.

This interim of war time places a shining light of hope and aspiration toward the future—the promise toward which we look.

26

HIROSHI NAKAMURA

ALICE HASN'T COME HOME

Teru was already in bed when the dinner gongs began to ring wildly.

Ever since the strike, two strokes meant a block meeting, three strokes meal time, and a continuous ringing such as now a riot or a serious emergency.

She heard subdued voices outside. Excited voices.

"Something's happened," Tad said. He pulled on his clothes and hurried out.

Mr. Noguchi herded him back. "Tadao, you stay home."

"What's happened?" Sally asked.

"Alice hasn't come home. No one has seen her since four o' clock."

"I thought Mrs. Sakaguchi looked worried when she came after supper and asked if Alice was here," Sally said.

"Are you going to search?" Teru asked.

"Yes," Mr. Noguchi said. "Tonight, we will ask for a few volunteers from among the young men only, but we are letting the people know so they will be ready to start out early tomorrow morning. Do we have a flashlight?"

"No," Teru said. "Remember, we gave them both to Mr. Johnson after it was announced that flashlights over two cells were contraband. We were afraid to keep the small one we had."

"Those were terrible times." Ayame sat up in her cot. Her eyes were fearfully wild and her hair spilled in disorder down her shoulder. "We were so afraid you would be arrested."

Mr. Noguchi looked at her sorrowfully. "You women better go back to sleep. Teru, fix your mother's hair for her."

"Is Paul going to search, too?" Tad asked anxiously. "Can I go?"

"No," Mr. Noguchi said. "No boys are going tonight. You can help tomorrow morning."

He joined the men outside. They could hear his precise voice raised in command. "This group will cross the slough and search due west."

Their footsteps tramped quickly away. Silence followed briefly. The voices went indoors. Teru and Sally crawled into their cots and looked at each other in the light streaming fitfully from the Maeda apartment. The burlap sacking hung outside the windows to keep out the summer sun was torn and needed patching. It flapped idly in the drafty air.

"I hope they find her," Teru whispered.

"I hope they do it before she—" Sally added quickly, "I hope she's all right."

"She is."

"They say that man from 226 was dead six hours when they found him the next day. That was summer though."

"Sally, stop it," Teru said, her voice rising sharply. They had found Mr. Nishijima curled up under a mesquite tree less than a hundred yards from the trail leading to camp.

"I'm sorry," Sally said.

"I'm sorry, too," Teru said. "I don't feel so good."

"Me either," Sally said.

The young men called to each other as they beat their way through the dark mesquite. They held their feebly flickering torches as high as they could and poked their flashlights here and there through the underbrush.

They gathered the full power of their young lungs to send their calls echoing into the darkness.

"A—lice!" . . .

Alice didn't know how long she walked. She followed the slough for a while, then crossed on some logs. The last ones she saw were Bill and Kate sitting on a blanket spread on the bank. They were too absorbed in each other to notice her as she circled around them.

She let the tears run unchecked down her cheeks as soon as she was alone and stumbling numbly forward, trying to get as far away from camp as she could. She didn't know when she left the trail leading to the river.

She nearly stepped on a rattlesnake and heard its warning rattle after she'd passed. She was unnerved and ran until her breath came in dry rasping gasps. She slowed to an exhausted walk.

Once she thought she saw the skulking form of a coyote through the mesquite and shivered. When she finally tripped over a protruding root to sprawl full length on the ground, she lay where she'd fallen, sobbing quietly, her face resting against the cooling sand.

She cried until she fell asleep.

She awoke and it was dark. She thought she could hear the faint clanging of a bell. She listened hard but she couldn't be sure. It was too dark to have been the dinner bell.

She sat up quickly and looked around and could see only the vague gnarled shapes of the mesquite trees. She stood up on unsteady feet.

Her mother must be worried. She had to go back. She gently rubbed her arms where they were bruised and torn by the mesquite thorns. She looked at the caked blood with surprise.

She looked around again and couldn't even tell which way she had come. She fought down a rising surge of panic. She wanted to run but couldn't make up her mind which way . . . what was it Gary had said when Mr. Nishijima had gotten lost?

"All he had to do was keep walking until he hit either the road connecting the camps or the river. It's only an hour's walk from the road to the river. If he happened to head north or south, he would have hit one of the trails leading from the camps to the river."

She remembered Bill had been there, too, saying, "Easy for you with your navigation training, but it's hard to go in a straight line through that mesquite. The first time we went to the river, we took almost three hours and we had a compass. There was no trail then."

"When we went, we missed the trail and spent over an hour looking for it."

Sammy Itaya said, "We didn't bring much water and we were scared."

Alice looked up. There weren't many stars. The North Star had some connection with the Big Dipper, but she couldn't even find the Big Dipper. She started to pick her way through the dense mesquite. The thorns and the protruding branches tore at her clothes and skin. She hit a clear spot and half ran across it. She stumbled ahead for what seemed hours.

The moon disappeared behind a cloud and she could barely see the sprawling roots and gnarled tree trunks underfoot. She finally stopped indecisively. What if she missed the trail in the darkness? She'd better wait until morning.

She sat down and felt the blood tearing wildly through her heart. The noise was deafening in her ears. The sweat stood out on her body and it was cold and clammy under her clothes. Her throat was parched and burning. She could taste the salt on her tongue. She must have been going in the wrong direction, she thought. She should have reached either the river or the road by now. She got up again. If she found the river, she would have water anyway. She could wait at the river until they found her. You could live a long time without food as long as you had water. Mr. Nishijima had died of thirst. Finding the road would still mean a long walk to camp before she could drink water. She'd better find the river first.

She started off again at right angles to the direction she had been following. There she thought the river was.

She was tired physically and mentally. Her mind wandered from the grim struggle to keep her feet going in as straight a line as possible.

How would she explain the impulse that made her walk so far away from camp? Her poor mother would be frantic by now. It would do her father good to suffer a little. The tears dropped off her cheeks leaving smudgy streaks behind.

What would she do when she got back to camp? She couldn't stay there. People would wonder why she'd run away. Why couldn't they mind their own business? You couldn't even have diarrhea without people knowing.

Every pregnancy was a block affair. She knew the routine herself. First the husband began to take home his wife's coffee and toast in the morning, Then he more and more frequently turned up at the laundry to do the washing.

Back home where their nearest neighbors had been two miles away, she'd wished there were more people around. Until assembly center. She changed her mind after that.

She shuddered at the memory of the terrible man who at first always managed to sit at the same table with them. She would still feel the impact of his ugly sensual eyes. His nostrils thinly flared like a pig's. His repulsive table manners. His plate held greedily to his thick slobbering lips. The food slurping up into his mouth. His tiny beady eyes never leaving her. The food curling in her stomach.

She remembered how they'd tried in vain to move when they discovered themselves assigned to the apartment directly facing the men's latrine. She remembered the men coming out of the latrine still buttoning their pants or hitching them to a more comfortable position.

She remembered how few people came to visit them and she had to suggest immediately visiting someone else whenever they did. How she lay half suffocating at night, her nose buried in the scratchy blankets. Her friends never lingering on the doorstep to talk and cut up the way they did at the Noguchi's or the Katai's. She and Paul and Emily and even seven-year-old Joan almost never staying home after the first few weeks and gradually taking to eating with whomever mealtime found them with.

The bitter night when she and Paul left their apartment before breakfast and stayed out until eleven that night. Their father flying into one of his rare rages and savagely lecturing them for two solid hours on behavior fitting to a Japanese. On family, filial piety, and conducting themselves at all times with pride and honor and an example to this rotten country . . . its racial discrimination, its eternal bragging, its self-righteousness. On Japanese being Japanese wherever they went and their solemn duty to spread Japanese wherever they went and the solemn duty to spread Japanese culture to the "eight" corners of the universe.

Are you proud to be an American now? After this so-called "humane" evacuation? This assembly center? This pigsty of a home?

Her own tearful flareup of emotion. Trying to make him understand. They HAVE to evacuate us. They had to do it in a hurry because Japan was all ready to invade California. These barracks are only temporary. This is an assembly center. Relocation center will be better.

Better? Where will we go from there? I had to sell our tractors and equipment to pay back the money I borrowed on this year's crop. The company took over the crop for the balance and it's like a weed patch now.

I'm a farmer. I can't farm without equipment or capital. I brought up you children somehow, because I was a farmer. How can I possibly support you working for day wages?

You don't think of those things when you talk so glibly of relocation and starting life all over again. As though I were still twenty-five and single instead of fifty-five with five dependents.

Assembly center had been like a bad dream.

She remembered the disillusionments. About acquaintances and even close friends. Discovering things that would never have come to light if they hadn't been thrown so closely together in camp. Only angels could stand the close scrutiny of barrack life.

Molly who had always seemed so sweet and good. Molly bawling out her mother for not leaving the apartment when her boyfriend came to visit.

Hearing things, ugly things, about people living right next to you. May was half-American, born while her mother had been working as a maid in San Francisco. Helen was half-Chinese, foisted, some said, on an unsuspecting husband who had enticed her away from home with a Cadillac and a thick roll of banknotes which she later learned were the joint property of fourteen other Filipinos. Pete was *Eta*. That's why he was so bitter and cynical about life. He was hard—hard like his body. Like his fingers digging into her flesh. Like the pains and shock that followed her limp surrender to his body.

She stopped and sat down to await the dawn . . .

Teru was awakened by her father's suppressed sneeze. It was still dark but she could hear people getting up next door. She heard her father saying to Tadao, "You help this morning, too."

They hadn't found Alice.

Teru threw off her blankets and swung her feet on the floor. It was cold and she dressed quickly.

"You girls don't have to get up yet," Mr. Noguchi said, but Sally was dressing, too. He asked Teru for a dry pair of trousers.

"You aren't going out again, are you?" Teru asked.

"I have to," he said, and he and Tadao left as soon as he had changed from his mud-caked trousers.

After breakfast, Teru and Sally stayed in the mess hall to help make sandwiches for the search parties. They searched all day and dragged the slough immediately below the camp.

They finally found her bruised and blood-soaked body on the second day near the river opposite Camp I.

JOE KURIHARA

THE MARTYRS OF CAMP MANZANAR

Dedicated to Messrs. Ito and Kanazawa

Within the great Owens Valley's desolate waste
Beneath the majestic peak of Mt. Williamson
In peace they rest, the martyrs of Camp Manzanar.
However bleak and forlorn be their resting place
The glorious sun forever shines on their graves.
Grieve not belov'd ones your fate, justice will right
As soldiers you died, as soldiers will be your rites.
On the sacred soil of our fatherland Nippon
Deified be your souls at Yasukuni Shrine.
In tears of sorrow we in unity divine
Pray that heavenly joys eternally be thine.
Sleep, dear ones, sleep! Sleep, in peace, sleep!

IWAO KAWAKAMI

THE PAPER

(the desert wind blows and sand covers the barbed wire posts—
    here was once a city a mile square: Topaz, "Jewel of the
    Desert"—a city of ten thousand people, aliens and citizens
    bound by barbed wires)
reconstruct now the first days of Topaz—
in the grayness following a sunset an old man shuffles along
    the road near the barbed wire fence
focus the lens of imagination upon an unshaven face
    beneath a shapeless straw hat—
    the face of a Japanese seventy years old
a blue working shirt—patched denim trousers—brown boots
    that rise and fall, leaving small craters in the dusty road
(this is the beginning of a Utah night and a wind springs up)
two pieces of paper start to flutter in the hands of the old man—
    his lips are moving
(what are you reading, sir? even if it is the camp's mimeographed
    newspaper it cannot be as absorbing as the sight of
    purple mountains resting on white sands of the desert)
this is a man who once had a celery ranch near San Diego—
he remembers the wet green stalks on frosty mornings
the Mexicans who said "La Golondrina" as they slashed at the
    roots with long knives
the imperturbable young Japanese American truck drivers

the fat Italian commission merchants who kidded him in a
    market jammed with vegetables
(war has forced an evacuation—harrows and discs begin to rust)
a sheet of paper flies out of the old man's hands
the wind carries it along like a white lifeboat bobbing in the
    middle of an ocean
a few yards beyond the fence the paper swerves to rest upon
    the sand
(regulation of the War Relocation Authority: all residents of
    the center are hereby warned not to go near the fence)
the old man stops, looks at the watch tower some distance away—
surely guards would not mind if he went after a piece of paper
slowly he walks toward the fence, bends down to go through
    the wires
a buzzard circles lazily above him—swings away in alarm
    as a shot shatters the silence of approaching night
dust rises in a cloud as the old man falls sideways in the road
the body twitches—grows still—blood seeps through the hole
    in the back of the heart
(order of the Military Police: fire if necessary if any resident
    is seen going through the fence)
a GI with a Garand runs down the steps of the watch tower
"Christ, was he trying to escape?"
he sees a mimeographed paper clutched in the dead man's hand
    but does not notice the wind beginning to push another
    piece of paper beyond the fence
(Topaz is now with Virginia City and Nineveh—the paper,
    buffeted by the rain and wind, has crumbled into dust—
    only the mountains and the desert remain)

29

NAO AKUTSU

SEND BACK THE FATHER OF THESE AMERICAN CITIZENS

Translated and Annotated for the White House by
Phillip W. Han and Edwin G. Beal
of the Library of Congress

Mrs. F. D. Roosevelt,
wife of the President of
the United States.
Washington, D.C.

Please excuse me, gracious one, for appealing to you directly for a special favor. My name is Akutsu; I am the wife of Kiyonosuke Akutsu. My husband came to the United States first on November 31, 1907. Since then he has been back to Japan twice. On May 17, 1919, he returned to the United States from his second trip to Japan. He has never gone back since then. He has been operating a shoe store at No. 422 Sixth Avenue, South, Seattle. It was at this store that he was arrested on February 21, 1942. He was arrested on the ground that he had subscribed for a magazine entitled "Fatherland" (Japanese title: *Sokoku*; this magazine is published in Tokyo). On March 19, he was transferred to Missoula, Montana, and on the last day of July it was decided that he was to be interned and sent to Louisiana. Now he is in Santa Fe, New Mexico.

My husband is an upright man, with no bad habits, such as smoking or drinking. He is a man of deeds, in which he surpasses even Christians. He was always mindful of our children's education, and worked hard to make them good (American) citizens of Japanese ancestry. In the first place, he has shown that he can advance by himself. In the morning he would get up at a fixed time, would open the store, and would begin his work. In the second place, he loved his children. At the dinner table, after returning home from his shop, he would inquire of the happenings of the day, and would say helpful things for the benefit of his family. Occasionally he would take the children out for a walk or for a trip. In the third place, he sometimes studied mathematics and history in order to be a good adviser to his children. Next he decided that it was not good to rent a house, for he feared that that kind of life might be an unsteady one. He thus acquired a lot and a two-story house at the corner of Tenth Avenue and Alder Street. He sent our eldest son to the Department of Engineering of the University of Washington, and our second son to Broadway High School.

It was on February 21, 1942, a frosty, cold day, that my husband was arrested on the ground that he had joined the "Society for the Fatherland." He never made any payment to the subscription department of "Fatherland," but he did pay one dollar and seventy-five cents, on November 17, 1939, to a customer of the store, who had begged him to buy the magazine. My husband did this because the man was a customer of his, and my husband did not want to lose his goodwill. We had no other intention. We did this once as we always would buy tickets for the dances given by firemen or policemen. After that we refused to purchase other issues, for we felt money was precious, and, besides, we had no leisure to read magazines. In any case, we had done it once for our customer. My husband, of course, was not a member of the society.

[Mrs. Akutsu describes struggling to sell the goods in the family's shoe-repair business for 20 cents on the dollar, then writing back and forth with the U.S. Attorney for Western Washington to seek her husband's release from the DOJ alien internment camp at Fort Missoula. —eds.]

On May 28, we received an answer from Mr. Pomeroy, who explained the results of the hearing conducted on April 3, 1942, at Missoula, Montana. He said that my husband had belonged to the Japanese Association (*Nihon-jin kai*), the Society for Japanese Military Virtue (*Nihon butoku-kai*), and the Buddhist Society (*Bukkyo-kai*). Furthermore, an old acquaintance of my husband had reported (to the authorities) that my husband was strongly pro-Japanese. But Mr. Pomeroy said that re-examination was possible if we could furnish another affidavit. He did not give the name of the person who had reported against my husband. What a bad fellow-Japanese he is! What a dirty man he is! I wonder whether he wanted to incriminate us and inflict hardship on our family, or whether he was just trying to get money. My husband might have said something for his homeland. But it is beyond my belief that he, who always dearly loved America and vowed not to go back to Japan, could say the type of thing he is reported to have said. He has lived in America for over thirty-five years, and America is his second home. Besides, America is the country of his children. Three times after being interned, my husband expressed his determination that he would not go back to Japan, because he loved this country. . . .

We do not know what to do. We have no way of having my husband's case re-examined. We feel sad to think that our efforts for an entire year have failed. This is why, as a last resort, I am writing this letter to ask you a favor. I am already fifty-six years old and cannot write English. I appeal to you with this Japanese letter, though I realize that it is impolite of me to do so. People who have advisers and good guarantors have come back (from internment). I have two children, and they work earnestly in this Center. Since the outbreak of the war, I have constantly been hoping to do something useful.

After hearing about the making of afghan squares, I decided that this was what I should do. I bought ten dollars' worth of wool, knitted afghan squares, and sent them to the Red Cross Branch in Seattle. I have devoted about one hundred hours to knitting in a Baptist Church. I also have joined the Parent-Teachers' Association. On February 21, when the F.B.I. agents came, I was knitting afghan squares. They asked for whom I was doing it.

As a housewife I have been under the protection of this country for twenty-four years. On October 15, my husband sent us a picture of himself. He has become thin, like a sick man, during the one and one-half years. It is probably due to his worrying about his family. He has no intention of going back to Japan. In line with the principle of not breaking the home, I appeal to you to send him back, after examining the events of the past year. The father is necessary for the education of the children. I appeal to you to send back the father of these American citizens and my honest husband as soon as possible. If you do this, I shall not trouble you again. I beg this of you.

Humbly,

Nao (Mrs. K.) Akutsu

October 23, 1943

Registration and Segregation

STATEMENT OF UNITED STATES CITIZEN
OF JAPANESE ANCESTRY

1. ....
        (Surname)   (English given name)   (Japanese given name)

   (*a*) Alias ....

2. Local selective service board ....
                                   (Number)

   ....
        (City)   (County)   (State)

3. Date of birth................................. Place of birth ....

4. Present address ....
                    (Street)   (City)   (State)

5. Last two addresses at which you lived 3 months or more (exclude
   residence at relocation center and at assembly center):
   .... From .... To ....
   .... From .... To ....

6. Sex .... Height .... Weight ....

7. Are you a registered voter .... Year first registered ....
   Where? .... Party ....

8. Marital status .... Citizenship of wife .... Race of wife ....

9. ....
   (Father's name) (Town or Ken)   (State or Country) (Occupation)
                        (Birthplace)

10. ....
   (Mother's name) (Town or Ken)   (State or Country) (Occupation)
                        (Birthplace)

**In items 11 and 12, you need not list relatives other than your parents,
your children, your brothers and sisters. For each person give
name; relationship to you (such as father); citizenship; complete
address; occupation.**

11. Relatives in the United States (if in military service, indicate whether a
    selectee or volunteer):
   (*a*) ....
          (Name)   (Relationship to you)   (Citizenship)

   ....
   (Complete address)   (Occupation)   (Volunteer or selectee)

DSS Form 304A
(1-23-43)

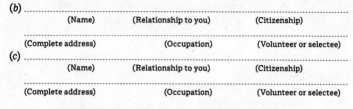

(b) ....
       (Name)   (Relationship to you)   (Citizenship)

....
(Complete address)   (Occupation)   (Volunteer or selectee)

(c) ....
       (Name)   (Relationship to you)   (Citizenship)

....
(Complete address)   (Occupation)   (Volunteer or selectee)

(If additional space is necessary, attach sheets)

12. Relatives in Japan (see instruction above item 11):

....
       (Name)   (Relationship to you)   (Citizenship)

....
       (Complete address)   (Occupation)

....
       (Name)   (Relationship to you)   (Citizenship)

....
       (Complete address)   (Occupation)

13. Education:

Name	*Place*	*Years of attendance*
(Kindergarten)		From .... To ....
(Grade school)		From .... To ....
(Japanese language school)		From .... To ....
(High school)		From .... To ....
(Junior college, college, or university)		From .... To ....

....
(Type of military training, such as R.O.T.C. or Gunji Kyoren)   (Where and when)

....
(Other schooling)   (Years of attendance)

14. Foreign travel (give dates, where, how, for whom, with whom, and reasons therefor):

....
....
....

15. Employment (give employers' names and kind of business, addresses, and dates from 1935 to date):

....
....
....
....

16. Religion .... Membership in religious groups ....

17. Membership in organizations (clubs, societies, associations, etc.). Give name, kind of organization, and dates of membership.

18. Knowledge of foreign languages (put check mark (✓) in proper squares):

(a) Japanese Good Fair Poor

Reading ☐ ☐ ☐

Writing ☐ ☐ ☐

Speaking ☐ ☐ ☐

(b) Other .... Good Fair Poor
(specify)

Reading ☐ ☐ ☐

Writing ☐ ☐ ☐

Speaking ☐ ☐ ☐

19. Sports and hobbies ....

20. List five references, other than relatives or former employers, giving address, occupation, and number of years known:

(Name)	(Complete address)	(Occupation)	(Years known)

21. Have you ever been convicted by a court of a criminal offense (other than a minor traffic violation)? ....

Offense	When	What court	Sentence

22. Give details on any foreign investments.

(a) Accounts in foreign banks.   Amount, $ ....
Bank .... Date account opened ....
(b) Investments in foreign companies. Amount, $ ....
Company .... Date acquired ....
(c) Do you have a safe-deposit box in a foreign country? ....
What country? .... Date acquired ....
Contents ....

23. List of contributions you have made to any society, organization, or club:

Organization	Place	Amount	Date

24. List magazines and newspapers to which you have subscribed or have customarily read:

....
....
....
....
....

25. To the best of your knowledge, was your birth ever registered with any Japanese governmental agency for the purpose of establishing a claim to Japanese citizenship? ....

   (a) If so registered, have you applied for cancellation of such registration? ....
   (Yes or no)
      When? .... Where? ....

26. Have you ever applied for repatriation to Japan? ....

27. Are you willing to serve in the armed forces of the United States on combat duty, wherever ordered? ....

28. Will you swear unqualified allegiance to the United States of America and faithfully defend the United States from any or all attack by foreign or domestic forces, and forswear any form of allegiance or obedience to the Japanese emperor, or any other foreign government, power, or organization? ....

---   ---
          (Date)   (Signature)

30

TOPAZ RESIDENT COMMITTEE

WE RESPECTFULLY ASK FOR IMMEDIATE ANSWERS

We, the citizens of the United States of America, residents of the Central Utah Relocation Project, Topaz, Utah, in order to perform our duties as loyal citizens of the United States and in order to uphold the principles of democracy as established in the Constitution of the United States do hereby state that:

Whereas, we the citizens of the United States have been asked by our Government to pledge our unqualified allegiance to this country.

Whereas, we have accepted in good faith and in full cooperation the extraordinary orders of the United States Army.

Whereas, we feel that we have given our fullest cooperation to this program of evacuation.

Whereas, we have temporarily surrendered many of the rights and privileges of citizenship which we have heretofore enjoyed.

Whereas, the Government through the Federal Reserve Bank has promised us full protection from unscrupulous people at the time of evacuation.

Whereas, we believe the Federal Reserve Bank has failed to protect the people.

Whereas, we suffered losses of homes, properties, work,

freedom of movement, separation from friends, and all things we felt dear to us without protest.

Whereas, we wish to prevent in the future, the mass evacuation or confining of citizens without trial.

Whereas, we feel that there is only one class of citizenship in this country and a loyal citizen of one race should not be treated any different from another.

Whereas, we believe that some of these things mentioned above constitute a violation of our civil rights.

And whereas, we believe sincerely and honestly in the principles of freedom of Speech, freedom of Worship, freedom of the Press and freedom of Assemblage as embodied in the Constitution and its amendments.

Therefore, be it resolved:

(1)   That we ask Secretary of War Henry L. Stimson that after a thorough investigation by the military Intelligence and the Federal Bureau of Investigation and other Federal authorities that persons that are cleared should have absolute freedom of movement and the choice of returning to their homes.

(2)   That we request President Roosevelt to give us assurance that he will use his good office in an endeavor to secure all constitutional and civil rights as American citizens.

(3)   That the security for the isseis be assured.

(4)   That we ask President Roosevelt to use his good office to bring favorable impression to the public regarding the loyal citizens.

(5)   That we ask that those isseis considered by the Government as being not disloyal to this Government be classified as friendly aliens.

(6)   That we have the Government note the advantages of the good publicity to be gained by disbursing nisei soldiers into the Army at large rather than by forming a separate combat team; and that the Government further note that the education of Caucasian soldiers can be made through deep comradeship that grows between soldiers facing a common task and thereby educate the American public.

(7) That the Government recognizing that we are fighting for the Four Freedoms as embodied in the Atlantic Charter should apply these democratic principles to us here at home.

(8) That we believe that if satisfactory answers can be given by a Government spokesman, preferably the President of the United States, to these questions we can go and fight for this our country without fear or qualms concerning the security of our future rights.

And be it further resolved, that we respectfully ask for immediate answers to the questions in this resolution.

[At Tule Lake, the Kibei in Block 4 translated this resolution into Japanese and adopted it with this addition to paragraph 8. —eds.]

In the event that we are not given satisfactory answers, we take it that our rights provided for by the Constitution are not being protected and understand that there is no reason for us to register without being provided with any information we should have regarding our citizenship.

31

KENTARO TAKATSUI

THE FACTUAL CAUSES AND REASONS WHY I REFUSED TO REGISTER

When registration ensued in the Tule Lake Relocation Center, I was aiding registration by interpreting and filling out the registration forms (form 126A-form 134A) for the registrants. . . .

A week had elapsed since the inception of registration but the number of evacuees appearing voluntarily for registration was negligible. Many were suspicious of the real intentions of the army or the W.R.A. There were rumors that spoke of soldiers forcing the evacuees into their jeeps and taking them to the administration building and making them register. There were whispered stories of how a nisei girl would be shipped away and required to work in a negro hospital if she signed "yes." There were conjectures about having our properties "frozen" by the government—that they would use our signed papers as a means to that end. That they would use our signed statements in any way they so desired. There were persons who definitely declared themselves that they had been "duped" by the W.R.A. That when they had registered "no"—found their "no" answers changed to "yes," when they appeared at the administration building to demand the return of their signed registration papers. They explained that they wanted their papers back because from the uncertain rumors circulating then, they had decided it was safer not to have signed "anything." Above all this confusion and dilemma an announcement printed on paper issued forth from the project director, Mr. Coverly. The announcement stated that if a father of an American citizen nisei should advise his son or daughter against registration—his punishment for such a crime would be twenty-years imprisonment and ten-thousand dollars fine. The camp's reactions to this pungent declaration was similar to a lazy easy-going horse abruptly bitten by an enterprising bee. The residents assumed that any person who advised or conspired in a body or group against registration was also in the same category and liable to the same punishment.

About eight days after the commencement of registration there occurred an incident that many of us will not forget for a long time. An army of soldiers surrounded Block 42 and at bayonet points, plus light machine guns, captured thirty-five boys of that block. I have heard about this occurrence from an eye-witness. Tears swelled my eyes as I heard his description of the heart rendering scene. Where little brothers and sisters clung tenaciously to their departing brothers, tearfully hysterical in their demand to wish to accompany them. Old men stood by helplessly, their eyes wet, dimmed, their lips hard pressed by angry teeth. Mothers pathetically waved farewells to boys whom they never expected to see again, their choked voices bade the boys "to take care of themselves—good bye." Some men raised their voices above the tumult of the crowd and shouted lusty "Banzais" to impart to the departing boys that they would not be forgotten. All the residents of the near-by blocks attracted by the commotion in Block 42 massed there and witnessed this distressing sight. Those that saw this Commando style method of the army, hustling their prisoners into their trucks, were embittered with an impression that cannot easily be dismissed from their minds. As proof of this; Ward 5, which is the blocks adjacent to Block 42, was nearly one-hundred per cent in its refusal to register. The other Wards in camp were not so well impressed so consequently they nearly all registered.

The reason the thirty-five boys were apprehended by the army was because the boys had signed a statement absolutely refusing to register. They had taken that signed statement to Mr. Coverly and presented him with it. They had caused no disturbance or violence while performing this act. They returned home safely that day and the army descended upon them the following night. As I look back now I think Mr. Coverly's predilection was to "throw a scare" into the populace and inclined to the belief that "fear of the consequences" would force the residents to register. Compared to the accomplishments of the other relocation centers, Mr. Coverly's methods resulted in a dismal failure of registration at Tule Lake.

These people had evacuated the Pacific coast peacefully and obediently because they were instructed by the defunct J.A.C.L. that to do so was to aid America in her war effort. Their beloved homes and livelihoods were swept away as if by a whirlwind tornado. . . .

After all their hardships, the populace of Tule Lake was stirred with indignation at the army's unnecessary method of apprehending the boys of Block 42. Needless to say, I was aggravated too. I decided not to register. If they were treating those boys like prisoners for refusing to register—then I would join them too. With deep conviction in the righteousness of my cause and with a firm reliance on the protection of divine providence, I acted against registration. To the humanity living in a normal American community, the beliefs and actions of the evacuees in the centers may sound and appear mediocre but to us, the residents of the centers—our hopes, our misfortunes, our troubles appear immense because we are part of its life and existence. Those thirty-five boys taken at bayonet points were not just a couple of dead-end kids—they were a symbol of our resentment against oppression. The suppressed emotional bitterness that was boiling upwards had to have an outlet and this was it. Many Japanese young men who in normal life would have been ashamed at their own rash actions took the opportunity to bash a few heads in. It did not matter whether they had proof or not—just a hearsay was enough. Inus, dogs or suspected stool pigeons, were attacked hither and yon. The once quiet camp of Tule Lake was thrown into a pandemonium. I heard that even a minister was assaulted. Oh well, I guess in these days of ammunition-passing preachers anything can happen.

The supreme court may pronounce the military evacuation of the Japanese from the Pacific coast legal, but there are some things that are not, cannot be ably controlled by judicial connivances and that is human emotions and reason.

My brother had volunteered and enlisted in the American army almost a year before Pearl Harbor. For my brother's sake and because America is my birthplace, I harbor no ill will towards this country. I am classified as a Kibei and labelled a pro-Axis. It is strange indeed to be gazed upon with suspicion when I am not in a position to do harm. I have never published propaganda, nor organized a "Bund" or spoken against the government of the United States while living in Seattle those many years. My father, mother and sister are now residing in Japan, that is the basic reason why I will not fire a gun against Japan. Of a certainty I will gladly work for America on the production front but I will not bear arms against my father's country. I will not bear arms against America either.

32

SADA MURAYAMA

LOYALTY

I am a citizen—
Let no slander
Slur my status.

In the other war,
I stood with countless others
Side by side
To fight the foe.
My arm was just as strong
My blood fell
As bright as theirs
In defense of a new world
More precious far
Than any tie of land or race.

If in this holocaust
It be decreed
My loyalty be tested
By submission,
What is the difference
If the end be same?

My reason may be tested—
Not my heart.

O, what is loyalty
If it be something
That can bend
With every wind?

Steadfast I stand,
Staunchly I plant
The Stars and Stripes
Before my barracks door,
Crying defiance
To all wavering hearts.

I am a citizen—
I can take
The bad with good.

33

MITSUYE YAMADA

CINCINNATI

Freedom at last
in this town aimless
I walked against the rush
hour traffic
My first day
in a real city
where

no one knew me.

No one except one
hissing voice that said
dirty jap
warm spittle on my right cheek.
I turned and faced
the shop window
and my spittled face
spilled onto a hill
of books.
Words on display.

In Government Square
people criss-crossed
the street

like the spokes of
a giant wheel.

I lifted my right hand
but it would not obey me.
My other hand fumbled
for a hankie.

My tears would not
wash it. They stopped
and parted.
My hankie brushed
the forked
tears and spittle
together.
I edged toward the curb
loosened my fisthold
and the bleached laced
mother-ironed hankie blossomed in
the gutter atop teeth marked
gum wads and heeled candy wrappers.

Everyone knew me.

CONFIDENTIAL STATEMENT TO DILLON MYER
DIRECTOR, WAR RELOCATION AUTHORITY

January 14, 1943

The problem of segregating "loyal to America" Japanese from those who are "loyal to Japan" in the ten relocation centers under the jurisdiction of the War Relocation Authority is a difficult one which is complicated by many factors.

To us, there is no question that immediate and summary action must be taken in order to assure those who are loyal to this country that un-American activities and utterances will not be tolerated by this government. On the other hand, as neither "free speech" nor "free assembly" should be abridged, some appropriate determination must be made where the legitimate bounds of our constitutional liberties end and subversiveness begin....

Before evacuation, we believe that most of the first-generation Japanese nationals were at least passively loyal to the United States. After all, they had spent the greater part of their lives here, had made a living here which was far superior to that which they could have enjoyed in their native land, and had reared their children with the underlying idea that America would be equally "good" to them. As for the American Japanese, we believe that, previous to the exclusion orders, practically all of them were one hundred per cent Americans. Most of them never thought of themselves as anything but Americans equal to any other American....

Notwithstanding these difficulties, it seems imperative to us that immediate action should be taken in every center to "pull out" those who are constantly agitating against this government or its representatives, or fomenting dissension and violence. The people in the center must be convinced beyond all doubt that the government means to protect the loyal and to enforce law and order at all times and for all persons....

Although the situation is well advanced in most of the centers, we believe that immediate action should be taken whereby, without warning or hearing, known agitators and troublemakers are moved out of the relocation centers and placed in special camps of their own....

In view of the fact that practically every person who has been "beaten up" in the centers is a member of our Japanese American Citizens League, many of our members have written in suggesting that our organization create special "gangs" for the protection of our own membership. They feel that strong-arm tactics should be met with the same kind of measures, as the government seems unwilling or unable to cope with this situation. Naturally, we have strongly disapproved such methods which borders on "taking the law" into their own hands. We have asked them to send in their suggestions to curb the alarming growth of gangsterism in the centers.

The unanimous consensus of opinion is that the WRA ought to take immediate steps to segregate the known agitators. Most of our chapter leaders have signified their willingness to name those whom they consider inimical to center welfare if their own names are not revealed. The names which they might submit could be checked with others who are reliable and who are not members of the JACL, in order to insure against possible prejudices simply because of organizational differences. . . .

The first step, then, as we see it, is to remove all the known agitators and troublemakers.

The second step is, we believe, to invite all persons, citizens and aliens alike, who desire repatriation to Japan either as exchange prisoners or deportees after the war, to declare their intentions in writing. These people should be moved to another special camp reserved just for people like themselves. . . .

The third step, we believe, is to place men who are trained investigators, such as FBI, Military, or Naval Intelligence agents, in the centers in some administrative capacity which will permit them to ferret out those who are disloyal and to arrive at some satisfactory arbitrary method of mass segregation, if that is necessary. . . .

We are not suggesting a reign of terror, or a witch hunt. We are merely calling for the same type of specialized investigation to prevent sabotage and espionage within the centers as that which is carried on on the outside.

The fourth step, we believe, is that people trained in administrative police and detective work be placed in charge of the internal security departments and that these administrators be more cautious in the selection of their departmental personnel. . . .

We believe that the four steps suggested will go a long way toward solving the problem of "mob violence" in the centers. . . .

Respectfully submitted,

JAPANESE AMERICAN CITIZENS LEAGUE

/s/ Mike Masaoka

MIKE MASAOKA
National Secretary

34

KAZUO KAWAI

(as Ryōji Hiei)

THIS IS LIKE
GOING TO PRISON

Translated by Xavi Sawada

After a journey of two days and two nights, the train arrived at its destination concentration camp. The mountain range in October had a thin, snowy tinge, the air in the basin was pleasantly cool, and the sun was already quite high. Some four hundred passengers stuck their heads out of the windows and looked around curiously. The line of gray huts was nothing new to them, but they stared in horror at the neatly assembled pyramid-shaped tent barracks next to the seemingly endless buildings, and at the tanks and jeeps placed menacingly at the entrance, surrounded by an iron fence. There was a kind of abnormal feeling. The tangled emotions of entering a new life—curiosity, fatigue, hope, rebellion—ran through their minds. The last roll call on the train was over and it was, finally, time to enter the camp.

Military policemen, bayonets on their shoulders, were looking in all directions. The passengers, all holding their own bags, boarded designated trucks. Kawamura was placed in a building with the fifty or sixty others who had been in his freight car. It had been built recently, perhaps to use as a school. The still incomplete rooms were barren and quite cold. Kawamura, who was dressed for warm weather, stood trembling. The others also looked cold. They had transferred from a camp in the middle of a hundred-something-degree desert, so it was an abrupt change in climate for them.

The luggage inspection began. They spread out their bags in front of two military policemen. Magazines, makeup, clothes, and other everyday items in bags of various sizes were individually inspected. Radios, typewriters, and sewing machines were given a particularly scrupulous inspection. Cardboard and wood suitcases, wrapping cloths, belongings of all kinds went this way, flew that way. An old man in the corner furtively removed an important document and hid it in his pocket. Some men were nodding off, exhausted from the wait. None of them, having gone through so many inspections, would have made the blunder of packing a prohibited item. Some had their belongings glanced at, flipped over, even closely inspected, but there was no trouble and they passed through quickly.

Some of the people who had been transferred to the camp before them were forming crowds and peeping through the windows. Some slipped under the guards' line of sight, ducked under the iron mesh demarcating the no-entry area, and called out, "———san," "———san." They spoke to each other by opening the double-paned glass doors, which would let in a sudden gust of cold wind.

Some voices could be heard saying, "I'm in ——— barrack, put in a request so you can live there too." Kawamura glanced around to see if his close friend Mutō had come, but there was no sign of him. He was looking forward to seeing Mutō, whom he had not met in the two years since his eviction. They had arranged in advance that Mutō would prepare a room for him.

"Sister!"

"Goodness, Saburō!"

He turned around. His friend Kume's wife, Akemi, who had lived in his village, was crying, her face pressed against her brother's shoulder. The siblings had not seen each other in two years.

"This is my younger brother, this is Kawamura-san. We were in the same barrack."

Akemi introduced them while using a hand to wipe tears from her face, pale and swollen from crying. Her brother was a vigorous, young, ruddy Nisei. He was handsome and looked just like Akemi.

"I arranged a room, so give them this when you go to the housing department," he said, handing his sister a piece of paper. He then said in a preoccupied tone, "See you later, then," and left. He had a "worker" badge affixed to his chest.

The inspection was over and registration began. They were called one by one to the front of a desk. One went, another went, and Kawamura was left last in line. . . .

"What's your name?"

"Kazumi Kawamura."

"Birthday?"

"Thirtieth of June, 1921."

"Birthplace?"

"California, Stockton."

So went the exchange between Kawamura and the military policeman. Nobody was left in the room other than the two of them. Kawamura's suitcase lay lonesomely in the corner. Noisy voices came from the hallway. The voice of a crying child, the thudding of shoes as someone boisterously ran around. The military policeman remained unperturbed and kept a calm voice as he continued to compose his records. The questions were the same as those he had asked the previous man.

"Father's name?"

"He is still alive."

"Mother?"

"She is in the center in Arizona."

"Siblings?"

"They are both in Japan."

After signing the papers, Kawamura took the envelope he received along with his suitcase and went to room number two.

He stood in front of the camera when called. A bright beam of electric light illuminated his face for just an instant. His sleepless face, framed by angular cheeks and colored bluish black by his stubbly beard, was grotesquely projected into the open space. It was an unpleasant feeling. They took pictures of his front and profile and stuck the number 2952A on him. Next, he faced another military policeman, who recorded his height, weight, and facial features, took the envelope containing his family information collected earlier, and started typing up several pages. The room was terrifically noisy. Women's voices, men's voices, some young, some old, some speaking poor English, some fluent English. He held his languid head in his hands and gazed at them.

An old woman was having her fingerprints taken at the next desk. The military policeman had probably just enlisted. His unpracticed hands daubed black ink on all her fingers. She stared as if watching something horrific and fixed her fierce eyes on her own wrinkled fingers, then on his large, graceful, Caucasian hands.

"It will be over quickly," the military policeman said to her empathetically, smiling. Did she understand him, or did she not? She remained silent. There was no hint of a smile. First the left hand, then the right, her fingerprints were pressed one by one onto two sheets of paper. It may have been Kawamura's imagination, but her hands seemed to shake a little. No doubt she was thinking: to have your photo taken, your fingerprints taken, this is just like going to prison. She would have good reason to think that, Kawamura mused.

He stole a glance at the old woman. She had the swarthy, rugged face of a rural person in her seventies, with crumply wrinkles and a completely white head of hair. Her eyes were sunken and half-closed. When the fingerprint registration was over, she recited something under her breath while wiping oil on her fingers to remove the black ink. His head felt heavy, as he stared at that old, hunchbacked woman. His fatigue and hunger began to make him restless. He wanted to get out of that room quickly. He emitted a few yawns. All the faces around him were sapped of energy. The military policeman finally finished his typing, and Kawamura started toward the fingerprint station.

"Kazumi! Kazumi."

Startled, he looked back toward the voice and saw Mutō standing at the window.

"Hey, Mutō."

Kawamura felt nostalgic as he gravitated to the windowsill. Mutō had not changed a bit in two years. He was still the skinny, extraordinarily tall Mutō, smiling as always. Kawamura pried open the window.

"I looked everywhere but couldn't find you—turns out you were in this place. How's it going, are you well?" Mutō's clear voice brought back memories.

"It's not going so well, actually, they've made me wait so long I feel rotten," Kawamura answered from inside the room.

"Hey, what happened to your mom?"

"She's not here for a number of reasons, but let's talk about it after we're settled."

"I got a room for you, so give Housing my name and address. You can come immediately."

Mutō left.

Kawamura left the room after giving his fingerprints. Now came the last registration, during which each person received a room assignment. He was the last in a long line.

"Hey, let's ask for a room for all five of us."

"Who knows if they'll give us one."

"I've heard that the single men are all crammed into the Rec Hall."

"That can't be true. In any case, let's try our best to negotiate."

Five or six young men were talking to one another toward the front. He heard women's voices as well:

"It would be nice if I could get into a barrack with you girls."

"I hope I get the middle room."

Kawamura was, more than anything, glad he did not have to worry about a room. It would certainly be unpleasant to live with ten other unacquainted bachelors in the rec hall. Though the last camp was uncomfortable, it was sad to leave a familiar place that had been home for more than a year, to move to a new camp and new barracks, and have to live with strangers. The newcomers' modest hope was to be able to at least live with as many people as possible from their former camp.

The overcast sky had, at some point, started to allow cracks in the clouds, and now the sun intensely illuminated the tops of their heads.

Kawamura held his four allotted blankets and left the office, having completed his registration without incident. He rested in a squat at the back of a truck packed with suitcases and blankets. He felt relieved. Staring at the bleak, treeless landscape as the truck turned right and left through the barracks, he felt dejected, his head was heavy, his mind blank. He was overcome by sadness when he considered that he was separated from his mother and would now also live apart from Kume. But when it occurred to him that from now on he would begin a new life with his old school friends, a pleasant life with people he got along with, his hope for a new tomorrow also filled him with expectant joy.

35

NOBORU SHIRAI

THE ARMY TAKES CONTROL

Translated by Ray Hosoda

The administration could not leave the fall harvest in the field to rot. The food was too valuable. Since the administration could not depend on the workers in the Agricultural Division or anyone else at Tule Lake to bring in the harvest, it recruited help from the other internment camps. Volunteers were transported hundreds of miles to Tule Lake and housed temporarily in tents outside the camp. From there they commuted to the fields where they worked.

It was a regrettable situation. The strikers glowered at the strikebreakers from behind the barbed wire, but the strikebreakers would not look them in the eyes. None of the strikebreakers looked back. The strikers cursed, but the strikebreakers were too far away to hear them. For the majority of us not involved in the strike, it was a distasteful scene. They were both of Japanese ancestry, both confined to the internment camps, separated only by a barbed wire fence. No matter who was right and who was wrong, we observers felt devastated. As bad as it was, the situation soon became even more demoralizing.

A rumor sped through our camp that the strikebreakers were being paid a dollar an hour, the same as laborers outside the camp. Not only were they getting better pay, but they were also consuming our food. When the strikers realized that the strikebreakers were being treated better than they were, they could barely restrain their tempers.

Soon afterward, some of our internee police witnessed American soldiers removing food from our warehouse. The soldiers carried it out right under our noses, probably for the benefit of the strikebreakers. As soon as our police realized what was happening, they jumped the soldiers and bravely fought them in hand-to-hand combat. Unfortunately, they were no match for the soldiers, who flattened them in no time. Our police hightailed it out of there and burst into a meeting with their news. It was not every day that the beaten police interrupted a meeting in progress between Kai and his top men.

Without any hesitation, forty to fifty quick-tempered men dashed to the warehouse to protect our property. When they got there, a military tank was already waiting for them. Chief Best had ordered it and set a trap for the men. Instead of rushing to the rescue, every one of the men rushed into a "fishing net," so to speak. It was a clean sweep. They were all thrown into a tent outside the camp that served as a stockade.

Afterwards, the tank rumbled up and down the lanes between the barracks, shooting blanks aimlessly. Using a bullhorn, a soldier in the tank yelled a warning: "Stay indoors! Don't come out!" We internees were so shocked we could hardly believe our ears.

A succession of incidents ensued. These frightened the Caucasian workers so much that one by one, they quit their jobs and left the camp. Chief Best decided he would let the military manage the camp until order was fully restored.

HYAKUISSEI OKAMOTO

SEVERAL BRETHREN ARRESTED AFTER MARTIAL LAW WAS DECLARED AT TULE LAKE IN NOVEMBER 1943

Translated by Violet Kazue de Cristoforo

damatte shimatta ichiya ikusabanashi no ato robe

> silence fell one evening
> after talk of war
> around fireside

jeep shizuka ni hashiru roni moyuru hino akaki yoru

> jeep patrolling slowly
> stove is glowing
> at night

fuyuyo waga kata o tataku otoko no iro shiroku

> winter night
> pale faced man
> taps my shoulder

VIOLET KAZUE DE CRISTOFORO

BROTHER'S IMPRISONMENT

ino hanaya sunapparaya nihyaku yonichi

flowers on tule reeds and sandy flats
brother confined over 200 days

The November 4, 1943, warehouse incident, caused by reports of thefts of food for the internees by War Relocation Authority (WRA) personnel, resulted in confrontations and disturbances at Tule Lake.

Brother Tokio, an innocent bystander, had been asked to help restore order among the agitators. As he was about to do so, he was arrested by WRA Internal Security personnel and accused of taking part in the disorder. During a night of brutal interrogation he was cruelly beaten, and not only was he denied medical treatment for his injuries, but he was imprisoned in the "Bull Pen" of the camp stockade—a place of maximum punishment for serious offenders.

Following the occurrence army troops took over control of the camp and martial law was declared at Tule Lake.

Then came spring, the snow melted and the Tule reeds sprouted and grew. By July the reeds even had blossoms. Brother Tokio was still confined in the "Bull Pen," after nine months of imprisonment without trial or a hearing. Fall was about to come again and, under those conditions of dark uncertainty and desperation, everything was measured in terms of the growth and death of the Tule reeds.

TATSUO RYUSEI INOUYE

HUNGER STRIKE

Translated by Masumi Izumi

FRIDAY, DECEMBER 31, 1943— HUNGER STRIKE

MORNING: Grapefruit, coffee, biscuit, mush
LUNCH: Rice, a small amount of sardines, tea
DINNER: Nothing (hunger strike)

The armed soldiers forced us to answer roll in the snow.
On the last day of the year, we started a hunger strike.
We ate some snow to fill our stomach.
Our guts are filled with Japanese spirit.
We do not cry from our lack of food.
We are angry at their ignorance.

—Poem by Hyakutaro Mori

. . . At 4 o'clock, the army threw some bread into the gate and left. No one went out to get them. Snowflakes fell on the bread, and the searchlights from the guard tower directed their beams on the bread. We commenced upon a fast. It was our only alternative, whether we liked it or not. We had checked the kitchen refrigerator. It was completely empty. The sardines, which had been left over from lunch, were all taken. The *shoyu* keg had been left behind because it was too heavy. The cabbages, being pickled for *tsukemono*, were also left behind because we had placed large coals on top to weigh them down.

The nurses were watching us from the hospital window. We signaled to them by turning the electric lights on and off. Showa 18 (1943) is about to come to an end any minute now. In reflection, so many things had happened this year. It has been an interesting experience, waiting for the New Year in the stockade. One man was released—a curfew violator. Another man was moved to the tent stockade, and another, to the hospital.

Total now is 196.

Letter from Yuriko:

I hope you won't catch a cold. Everyone is well at our place. I still feel headachy so I will stay in bed as much as I can. I drank some Wakamoto (medicine for my stomach). I started to wash clothes but since I feel badly I decided to leave it for a while. The children are okay and want to play outside but I'm going to keep them in until New Year's Day. I hope you will come back by New Year's, as we are really lonesome. All the neighbors are really nice to us. We don't know how to thank them.

Mr. Good sent us candy, nuts and homemade cookies. The neighbors cleaned the house, went to the post office and brought coal for our house. It was really helpful. Masami and Mr. Hayashi are the only ones in their families that are well. Mrs. Hayashi helped us so much that now she caught a cold and is sick in bed. The children sleep every night with their dolls. Did you receive the pipe?

I felt fine, as long as the children were healthy. . . .

SHOWA 19 (1944)

SUNDAY, JANUARY 2, 1944

Snow—Hunger strike.

Two men fell sick last night (heart trouble), so we called the doctor—he is called a doctor but actually has only graduated from nursing school. After a long wait, he came. One of the two men was suffering from chest pains, and they were both sweating heavily. They appeared to be in a lot of pain. One of them is an elderly man, who had been hospitalized for half of last year due to a serious illness. We asked the doctor to take them to the hospital, but he kept saying he didn't have that authority.

Doctor: "You are asking for something I cannot do. You insist on the impossible. What if I asked you to present me with a million dollars? Can you do that right here?"

Inouye: "Yes, I can."

Doctor: "Fine. Then, do it."

"Here it is," Inouye said, pounding on his chest. "There is nothing more valuable than life."

The doctor remained silent. . . .

After roll call, they came to take away Mr. Kuratomi. One soldier asked one of the men, who hadn't come out for roll call, "Did you sign the resolution? Were you forced to sign?"

The man answered, "No, never. We are all of one spirit."

Soldier: "Why didn't you come out for roll call?"

Man: "I feel dizzy when I stand up."

Soldier: "What do you think will happen if you keep refusing to eat?"

Man: "We will continue our hunger strike until we die."

Mr. Yamamoto informed the hospital about the hunger strike. Apparently, Mrs. Yamamoto had also heard about it and came to the fence. She shouted to her husband, "You will die if you don't eat."

Mr. Yamamoto: "I'm all right. I won't die that easily. Please inform the camp residents about what is going on."

Mrs. Yamamoto: "Okay."

Kuratomi came back in about one hour later. He had met with the FBI and Captain Hartman, and he shared the following conversation he had had with them:

Interrogator: "What will you do if you have someone falling sick from fasting?"

Kuratomi: "If we have people falling sick, the army is responsible for that. We will continue fasting, not only until people get sick but till we have people dying, unless you release us to the camp."

Interrogator: "Do you expect to win against the army?"

Kuratomi: "This is not about winning or losing. If we lose, we simply die."

Interrogator: "Are you serious?"

Kuratomi: "When a Japanese enters into a resolution, he will not go back on his word."

Interrogator: "What do you think of the fact that the camp residents are keeping quiet?"

Kuratomi: "That is the calm before the storm. You might not understand the Japanese psyche, but the people are about to explode."

As we were listening to Kuratomi, soldiers returned Tsuda, Yoshiyama and Uchida from the tent stockade to the barrack stockade. The time was 4:30 p.m. Kuratomi had told the captain that it was about time the army realized how mistaken they were and how they were putting themselves in trouble. He also told him about all the theft committed by the soldiers.

In response to Kuratomi, Captain Hartman had said, "The army doesn't care whether you eat or not." He also added that Austin was extremely upset about our hunger strike. . . .

The FBI agent had asked Kuratomi, "Do you think a hunger strike is a good idea?"

Kuratomi had answered, "I don't know if it is a good or bad idea, but this is the only way left for us to protest. If you have a better idea, tell me." The FBI agent had remained silent. I ate a little amount of garlic.

BUNICHI KAGAWA

GETA

Translated by Junko Kobayashi

When I peeked into the boiler room of the block, I saw scattered cards of gently refined flower images of *Ume* (plum blossom), *Sakura* (cherry blossom), *Kiri* (paulownia), *Momiji* (maple), and *Hagi* (bush clover) on top of the old table in the corner. People were playing cards to take their minds off their depression and frustration from living in camp. Although I am watching people play only when I have time, I have come to learn some of the common phrases associated with the card game of *hanafuda*: "flower cards," such as "*yama ga hikui*" (the stack is low), "*kame no teodori*" (turtle hand dance), or "*toshiyori no kuseni yoku okosu*" (for an old guy, you get lucky pick). I smile when I hear such phrases: it was here that I learned, for the first time, that the paulownia tree card was called *geta*. There is a *haiku* sensibility in this silly nickname. I found it fascinating, and appreciated its simple charm.

As for *geta*, I remember everyone was actively making *geta* soon after we were put in camp.

There was not a dime's worth of difference among different camps—all that could be seen was sand, cactus, and sagebrush. A glimpse of this bleak landscape told us all that we needed to know about what was in store for us. Manzanar, where we were first sent, was located in the middle of the desert. When we walked to the communal bath, the condition of the road was so bad that our feet were quickly covered in sand. Since we were wearing the slippers we had hastily packed in our luggage, it felt as if we were scooping sand using our slippers. We were sick and tired of sand. This might be the main reason that making *geta* came into vogue throughout camp, but nobody really knew who started it all. Even I, who am the king of clumsiness, picked up a piece of scrap wood, borrowed a saw and a hand drill, and after an enormous struggle managed to create a pair. When better-quality materials became available later, people started to inject great ingenuity into making *geta*. As a result, *geta* even began appearing in arts and crafts exhibitions in camp. And yet the utility of *geta* was the reason we made them. My own pair of *geta* was quite ugly. But there were even worse, the kind that could only barely be recognized as *geta* by the fact that they were being dragged around on someone's feet.

Older people were wearing *geta*, women were wearing *geta*, and children, too, were wearing *geta*. Here is Tomiko Kawasaki's *tanka* poem:

> in the early evening
> piercing red
> of *geta*
> at the foot of a small child
> accompanied by a mother
> to the bath

Yoi hayaku hahani sowarete furoniyuku osanagono geta akaku menishimu
「宵早く母に添われて風呂にゆく幼子の下駄赤く目に泌む」

As you can see from this *tanka*, even toddlers just learning to walk were wearing cute *geta* as tiny as peas. I experienced a strange feeling, as if I had again become fully Japanese once I put on my *geta*. I imagine that many of you might have felt the same way. Our lives started anew from the evening of our arrival in camp, as we unloaded our luggage in the assigned barrack. My mind was in a daze for a while, and indeed, I did not have a sense of who I was anymore. It was as if I had been emptied out.

We had just lost our homes, our savings, our properties. We had been stripped bare, separated from our families and without knowing where our friends were. With the chaos that the war had brought, we were thrown into such confusion and anxiety that we didn't have any idea of what we were doing anymore. With the tags dangling from our collars, like lost children, arms holding as much hurriedly packed luggage as possible, feeling the eerie glimmer of the bayonet, held by soldiers, who were supposedly protecting us, we were crammed into buses and trains in the rain, and sent to far, unknown places, which turned out to be in the middle of a desert, where we had nothing of ourselves to hold onto. We wondered what would happen to us. Tossed into the turmoil of war and what fate had visited upon us, we had the gloomy feeling that we had lost our way toward the future.

Geta seemed to bring us out of this state of stupor. How consoling and comfortable to feel one's bare feet slipping into geta. We felt a tremendous sense of solace and intimacy, with geta on our feet for the first time since coming to the USA. A pleasant sensation moved intensely through my body, as if I had returned to my childhood. It was the simplicity and subtle warmth that came from my geta. It reminded me of the fields and mountains back home. All of us felt a closeness because we were wearing geta. In a natural way, geta made us understand that we were Japanese. We were all in the exact same circumstances, and therefore we had to console and encourage one another from now on. Geta symbolized the life of Japanese who lived close to the earth, and it was the geta that had aroused in us a sense of affinity.

We all felt a sense of camaraderie. At night, some young men sung naniwabushi as they strolled outside in their geta. Others were almost always in geta, no matter where they went, be it to visit their friends or to go to the mess hall. Amid the kara koro sound of wooden geta as they walked, supporters of a noble cause made their demands at the camp administrator's office. I cannot count the number of times in the summer evenings when I looked up at the cloud-covered top of the majestic Sierra mountains as I was heading to the bath in my *geta*, a cotton *tenugui* draped on my shoulder. At times I could hear the sweet-sour twang of the *shamisen* floating from a barrack somewhere, pouring into and then dissolving into the sand.

Little by little, we calmed ourselves. We were still living in confinement, but the sharp edges of camp life were softened as we wove together the thoughts that emerged from deep inside our minds. Over time, some of the harshness was softened.

There were movies and talent shows. Outdoor music concerts were held under cool starry nights. Children started to play baseball and adults searched for rare wood in the mountains to create walking sticks and pipes. Without realizing it, they stopped thinking about the ordeals right after the confinement as they devoted themselves to their meticulous work. By that time, schools had been built. The Buddhist temple had gone up, as had the Christian church. At first, people had no choice but to walk the long distance to a mess hall in a different block and wait in a long line, but now they could have their meals in their own mess hall.

The quality of life in camp attained this level because we were able to regain a sense of who we were. Putting aside the circumstances—that we were seen as enemy aliens during wartime—we put forth our best effort to reconstruct our lives. What we managed to accomplish with our mere hands and feet permeated our environment. The landscape we constructed became visible even from the outside camp. The greater and more meaningful this accomplishment, the more appreciation we should feel to *geta,* which powerfully bestowed upon us a sense of support and connection.

It has already been three years since our life in camp began. During this time, we have experienced so many incidents and troubles, including the murder of the Co-op manager, the mess hall registration problem, the loyalty issue, the draft, and the segregation. Reflecting on what our feelings and thoughts have undergone, I believe these unfortunate happenings were a natural outcome. We had no way of stopping this process that has brought us to the present. Nevertheless, I cannot help but miss the early days of *geta*. I wish so many things had taken place differently, amicably. A harmonious attitude would have produced greater understanding and empathy, and we could have been better able to support one another. This was not an impossible dream. Without even realizing it, while engaging in discussions and arguments about camp controversies, we gradually distanced ourselves from the early feelings we had when we slipped on *geta*.

When it came to the feeling of wearing *geta*, there had been no distinction between young and old, nor between Issei and Nisei.

Volunteers and the Draft

40

MINORU MASUDA

A LONELY AND PERSONAL DECISION

The physical hardships [of camp] we could endure, but for me the most devastating experience was the unjust stigmatization by American society, the bitter reminder that racism had won again over the Constitution and the Bill of Rights, the perception that the American people had thrown us into concentration camps simply because of our blood. It was galling, infuriating, and frustrating. Scapegoats we were, and imprisoned scapegoats to boot.

At the same time, the stigmatization of being branded disloyal and imprisoned evoked a sense of shame, as if the wrongful branding and the unjust act were somehow valid because of its sanction by American society, an upside-down perception.

Added to the self-imposed cloak of shame was the altogether human defense of submerging anger and bitterness: allowing it to surface and bubble would bring forth pain too strong to bear and detract from the goal of survival and achievement in the postwar years.

Then, into this state of mind came the announcement that the army would be recruiting from the camp to form a segregated regimental combat team. The news fell like a clap of thunder on incredulous ears. How could the government and the army, after branding us disloyal, after stripping us of our possessions and dignity, and imprisoning us in barbed wire concentration camps, how could they now ask us to volunteer our lives in defense of a country that had so wrongfully treated us? The incredible announcement caused immediate turmoil and split the camp into two. One group reiterated the complete irrationality of the recruitment under these circumstances, and pointed out that once again the government was exploiting us and doing us in. The other group took the longer view and saw the threat posed to the future of the Nikkei if recruitment failed. A society as irrational and racist as the one that put us into Minidoka could as certainly be expected to follow by saying that the fact that there were no volunteers only proved their rightness in calling us disloyal and throwing us into camps.

I wrestled with the problem as both arguments tumbled around inside my head. It was a lonely and personal decision. I was older than the others. I was married, more mature, and had more responsibilities. It was a soul-searching decision, for the possibility of death in the battlefield was real, and, in the Nikkei context, almost expected. I admit, too, despite all the trauma, that an inexplicable tinge of patriotism entered into the decision to volunteer.

There were 308 volunteers for the 442nd Regimental Combat Team from the some six thousand to seven thousand people that were in camp [at Minidoka].

The rest of the story is history: our induction, travel to Camp Shelby, Mississippi, our training with the larger Japanese American volunteer contingent from Hawaii, then overseas and the combat record of the 442nd.

41

TAMOTSU SHIBUTANI

THE ACTIVATION OF COMPANY K

Company K, School Battalion, was activated on 25 July 1945 with 258 student enlisted men, three cadre NCOs, and one officer. When the men learned that the company commander was to be First Lieutenant Joseph Catalano, who had been the executive officer of E Company, groans of despair arose. The NCOs, who had had more contacts with him, insisted that he was "not a bad Joe," but the privates contended that he was "chicken shit." Had he not enforced all the petty regulations on the Turkey Farm? When they learned that Staff Sergeant Endo, a Texan who growled orders with a heavy drawl, was to be acting first sergeant, their unhappiness was compounded.

"Them two bastards ought to get along pretty good. That Endo is the worst Boochie noncom I ever saw. He's a bastard! He thinks his shit don't stink! And that fuckin' Catalano! Jesus, what a chicken shit bastard! I seen him stop a guy for not salutin' him. He chewed his ass for five minutes and then made him clean the can. He acts tough as hell too. Two of a kind, and we gotta have both of 'em for three months!"

It was bad enough to be in the leftover company without having a petty commanding officer and a first sergeant who could not get along with Nisei. . . .

The first day of school was one of utter chaos. The company marched to the school area in the rain, and after some confusion most students were able to locate their classrooms. The doors were locked. When they finally got inside, they discovered that there were no desks; each room contained only one or two chairs. Nor were there any instructors. The only things ready for use were the fluorescent lights on the ceiling and the blackboards.

"What the fuck is this? They make us come to school, and they tell us to hurry up so we can get overseas. And they got nothing ready."

"Jesus Christ! Why don't they clean up the fuckin' place? What do they expect us to do, sit on the floor?"

"Jesus Christ! It's cold in here. No stove! I don't see no radiator. Holy fuck! We're gonna freeze our ass off when it gets cold."

"Goddam! We always get the ass end of the deal. Boy, we been salty ever since we hit Fort Meade. I figured something like this would happen. Nothin' ready! How in the hell do they expect us to study in a dump like this? Look at them other guys. They got a nice warm building with Coke machines and everything else. They got nice desks and everything."

The teachers were almost a half hour late; they had been receiving instructions from the division chairman. They ordered the men to go to another building to get some tables and benches. Not enough seats were available, and during the morning several had to sit on the tables.

In all fifteen sections it became apparent from the beginning that discipline could not be enforced. When one of the instructors warned his students that if they did not do well, measures might be taken to make things more unpleasant, the reaction was hostile.

"Goddam! There you go already! Always threatenin'! What's the matter with this goddam place? All they do is threaten ya. No matter what you do they threaten ya. No wonder everybody's pissed off! That's why everybody wants to goof off. Lose fight!"

"What do you want to goof off for?" the sergeant retorted.

"It won't do you any good. You can't buck the army. You been in long enough to know that."

"Aw, hell. We didn't ask to be sent here. We got Shanghaied."

"Not all of you though. Some of you guys volunteered."

"That was a long time ago. Hell, I volunteered from camp, and they turned me down. That's what pissed me off."

"Anyway, this place is chicken shit. All they do is threaten ya."

An instructor in another section found his students even less responsive. He wrote a simple character on the blackboard and asked, "Kumamoto, what's that?"

"You got me, teach. I don't know Booch from nothin'."

Looking at his class roll, the sergeant continued, "Honda, you answer the question."

"Aw, what for you peek on me? How 'bout all dem other guys? Why me?"

"Listen! When I call on you, you stand at attention and recite. You're in the army."

"You like fight? Come, we go outside."

Teaching was impossible on the first morning. The instructor of section F-I kept reiterating that it was the best in the division. Each time he said this the reaction consisted of guffaws and hoots of laughter. The sergeants were unable to control their classes. No matter what they said, no one paid attention. Anyone who tried to enforce his orders was immediately challenged to a fight. The men talked among themselves or slept.

"Hell, we might as well go over now. We ain't gonna learn anything in this fuckin' place. The main thing is you gotta know how to fight or you'll stop a bullet. If Okinawa was so tough, you can imagine what it's gonna be like when they hit the mainland. Goddam! I'll bet them fuckin' Boochies'll be out there with bamboo spears and everything else. We won't be able to trust nobody in that place."

42

TOSHIO MORI

SHE IS MY MOTHER, AND I AM THE SON WHO VOLUNTEERED

"She's the mother of a dog," he heard.

He did not stop lathering himself. There were several under the shower with him talking among themselves. Apparently they did not hear.

Then he heard the voices in the latrine, but he could not make out who they were. "It is the duty of a parent to guide their children to right thoughts and action, and if a son should go wrong it is criminal that she does not reprimand him." The man was talking loudly.

"She is weak, without spunk," the other guffawed. "Her boy can be put into her eye and yet cause her no pain."

"Too bad her husband is dead. This is the result of an upbringing without a man in the family."

He strained himself to hear more but was unable to grasp the low mutterings that followed. Now he turned on the water and washed himself hurriedly.

If he could only get out of the shower quick enough and learn the identity of those men. They are Issei, he thought madly. What right have they to talk bad about his mother? What do they know about his family and what business is it of theirs? They don't want trouble for themselves but make trouble for others.

You volunteer and it becomes everybody's business. You volunteer and they think you've become a man-killer. You volunteer and they think you're stupid and foolish for jumping into the fire. You are hated and abused by the young who hate to go to war. You are accused of reopening the draft for Nisei and so you are the devil. You are seeking personal glory and commissioned ranks; you are the patented hero, American-made. You are sending others to butcher themselves to hell and gone. You are the despised who are diseased with the cancer to make war, to prolong war, to glorify war.

You are not a man of feelings; you are an automaton. You have no union with the people's thoughts and aspirations; you have not communed with anyone but with the selfish self. Yes, you are the traitor of your ancestors. You are the damned; you are the purveyor of evil; you are the carrier of mankind's pus.

When he came out of the shower no one was in the washroom. There was a peaceful air in the room, a lull that brought restlessness into his lean frame. He looked in the mirror—there was once an innocent, naive youngster in you, his image said. He was once pure as humans come; he was a child, once helpless, once a being who was all for the taking without a conscious greed. He was once an animal who did not know the game nor the man-made rules; he was the believer of yes for yes and no for no.

And now look at you—you are crafty; you are smart; you have fists; you have hate; you have brutal strength; you have lust; you have greed. You are green in the game but learning mighty fast. You are picking up knowledge—higher learning, and profitable, from the street. Better go easy there, Hiro Murata, citizen of the United States and of the earth. Think rationally, kid. Don't raise your blood pressure over little matters. There is to come the bigger things in your life. Store up your energy for your day of days. When it comes, shoot the works.

And about the conscience, young fellow. Who made you as you are today? Was it yourself alone or did time and environment make you? You are you now. You are wrong in many ways, and you are right sometimes. Say to the public, "Time made this man!" But have the guts, little man, when you come face to face with yourself to admit, hereafter, I become responsible for myself because I have eyes to see.

Go all the way, rookie. Follow through. Don't hesitate. You wouldn't hesitate if you're taking a cut at the ball, would you? You wouldn't stop to study whether you're biting at a bad one, would you? You would rest on your judgment, good or bad. Is it not so? You either swing or you don't. Life is a game too, and life is full of mistakes, old man—without and within. Don't get gray and old over mistakes—mistakes make you, you know, if you have taken a cut cleanly. Yeah, man, keep cool for now. Ask for time. The rest will come to you whether you like it or not.

Wearing his Topaz-made wooden clogs, Hiro now walked homeward. The south wind picked up the loose surface dust and skyward it swirled. He followed its pattern with a detached thought. Last year I would have exclaimed and damned the place. Now I lift my eyes for the direction of its path and see nothing startling about it. I am callous and blasé; therefore, I have grown.

His mother was waiting for him by the doorway, standing empty-handed and nervously.

"What's the matter, Mama? Isn't it time to get supper?" he asked, noting her unusual behavior.

"We're going to the mess hall tonight for supper," she said decisively. Her voice, though faltering, had a purpose.

"Okay," he agreed. Then he could not ignore her agitation. "Why, Mama? Are there some special doings in this block?"

"No. I am going there to give the block people a piece of my mind. I want to speak to them—explain to them that what we do is our affair. I want them to understand that we are not the kind of folks to stand for insults."

Oh, oh, he thought, knowing well her fury once aroused. Not now, Mama. Hold it a little longer. Allow me the opportunity. "No use, Mama. They talk behind our backs. Let them have their day. We'll have ours."

"I want criticism stopped," she cracked sharply.

Her obstinate temper cut his protest short. Has the time come already? he asked. Ready or not, we are it. Is this the time to prick the boil?

It was a normal day for the average diners, but for the Muratas it was a special one. They stood in the line with the rest in cafeteria style as they went past the serving counter. Some looked at them curiously but the majority was not aware of their presence.

His mother's eyes glittered with cold fury as he nervously talked to her. She is preparing herself for the occasion, he thought. She is steeling herself. Jesus Christ, it's going to be uncomfortable sitting in there. She has the gumption; she will spill everything. What a woman. Boy, these people will have a come-down.

He chuckled to himself, picturing the relaxed faces stiffening with the outburst. It could be funny; it could be nothing but funny to him at this time.

It was a meatless lunch as usual. They went to their table, their plates filled with carrots, potatoes, and onions cooked in shoyu sauce. On each table was a plate of lettuce salad. They took strong tea.

Before they had scarcely wetted their mouths, his mother approached the block manager, who made announcements for his block. Hiro saw him nodding his assent to Mama's request, and then he paid attention to his food.

The block manager rapped the triangle for attention. Here goes, he said to himself. He could see Mama standing beside him, fairly bursting with fire.

"Mrs. Murata wishes to address you people. You have the floor, Murata-san," said the block manager.

She was fairly cold and unprepared when she began. Her voice was trembling and high-pitched. "I have something to say to you folks. It has been on my mind for quite a while. I always like to keep matters straight, and if I should happen to hurt some of your feelings it is because you have wormed into my family's affair."

Hiro sat chilled in his seat. He squirmed and kept his eyes on the food. The room was still.

"My son, as you well know, volunteered for the United States Army. As this is the sore subject which alienates you people from us, I shall enter into our private affair once and for all. If you cannot understand us after hearing me—then—then we can do nothing to bridge our differences.

"I have heard many times, both directly and indirectly, the harsh criticism coming our way. And why do we receive this treatment? Simply because my son here volunteered for the Army. Before that, you counted us as one of you. Now, we are ostracized.

"As a mother I shall relate to you how I felt when he volunteered. When my son told me that he had volunteered for combat duty I broke down. As a mother I was thinking in terms of our personal life. I raised him so he could, in my old age, give me comfort and support. I did not want him to die. I wanted him; I needed him. It was cruel that he must go."

Now Hiro looked at his mother unashamedly. Her eyes were clear and piercing as she commanded attention. A hush fell over the people as she paused.

"Do not for one minute think that my boy plunged into this with youthful fervor. My friends and priests vainly advised him against leaving his mother behind. For days and weeks my boy withstood these men—thoroughly convinced of his convictions. And what is that—this conviction which some of you are attempting to destroy in a Nisei? He is as much a Nisei as you are an Issei. It may be unusual for an Issei to volunteer but it certainly is not when a Nisei does."

His eyes were glistening; drops of warm tears fell on his lap. He did not raise his head. Mother, Mother, he whispered. I did not think you understood.

"And what are his reasons for volunteering—volunteering from a concentration camp, if you consider it so? What makes him risk his hide when he does not have to? He volunteered, fellow people, because he does not know any country but this land. He does not know Japan; he does not know England nor Russia nor China. He does know the place where he was born and raised. He does know its familiar way of life, and don't tell me that that is unimportant. The way some of you Issei speak adoringly of your mother country shows what the early ties could do to individuals. Some of you cannot forget Japan, and here I mean the Japan of your childhood days—the cherry blossom festivals, holidays, the beautiful lakes and mountainsides, the quaint villages, the dragonflies and the cicadas in the summer evenings.

"So when my son responded to his country's call, he had memories and visions—just like you. He too has the smells, the sights, the flavors, the music that possess him. He is you— he represents you who are living and dying here. And those of you who are smiling amusedly because you are not going to die here but return to Japan, I ask you—why did you come to America? What was your purpose? Why did you remain? Answer me these with reason."

My mother is illiterate; she did not have a formal education, he thought. But she knows a hell of a lot more than these squirming gentlemen and ladies. She's having a field day here.

"My friends persuaded vainly. My son was unmoved. They told him that if he joined the Army he was going to die. Then he told them; my boy did. He said, 'I am going all right but I'm not volunteering to die—I'm a soldier who wants to live. Because I want to live I am volunteering.' He and those who volunteered want to live. They want themselves to live; they want their families to live; they want their families' families to live."

I am glad; I am glad for this day; I am glad that there was the time and place for all that occurred on account of my volunteering, he thought.

"Now, we are returning to the petty things—to the matters which make life unpleasant for us. If you still can't agree with us, will you please keep it to yourself? It is not your business if my son wishes to serve his country. It is he who is risking life—not you. And if he believes it is worthwhile, you or anyone else have no right to stop him—not even his mother.

"And mark my words, folks. These boys who serve for us, the people, they will be remembered in the annals of this country. They will be remembered as those who led the crusade for freedom and peace in behalf of their people."

There was not a sound in the room as his mother returned

to her table. He watched her sit down and peck at her food. Their plates were heaping full when they rose to go.

He walked with his head high. He could see their eyes following them. Yes, she is my mother, and I am the son who volunteered. Whatever she said, now I am responsible, his eyes and bearing said. If there is further ado, look me up. Gradually the clatter of knives and forks filled the air, but there was little laughter and talk.

He and Mama were first to leave the dining hall.

43

JŌJI NOZAWA

FATHER OF VOLUNTEERS

Translated by Andrew Way Leong

In the six months since Mr. Saeki had sent Masuo and Jōji to the army, he had aged so quickly that he now looked older than his years. He would get so lost in his thoughts that, at work, he would sometimes catch himself having drifted away, only to see everyone laughing at his startled look of surprise. The truth was that he already knew his heart wasn't in his work anymore. No, it wasn't just work, it was everything. Even his onetime obsession with playing *go* had dwindled to the point where he no longer wanted to look at a board.

When his sons told him they wished to enlist, insisting that this was not only their right as citizens but also their duty, he accepted their words as a matter of course. Mr. Saeki agreed with their thinking, so did not make any effort to object. He thought that he should do his best to respect his sons' determination. When the time came for them to leave, he took the day off and went with them all the way to the train station. Although he tried to stay in good spirits as he bid his sons farewell, when he saw how they were not just fulfilling their duty but also leaving the family behind, he was overcome with a sense of desolation that, try as he might, he could not just *gaman* away. "Duty," "loyalty"—as the feeling of those beautiful words floated into the air, he thought about his sons, about where they now stood, how he could never have imagined that they would become soldiers. This was when the worries began.

Mr. Saeki had allowed his two eldest sons to enlist, but he was comforted by the thought that at least Saburō, the youngest, wanted to stay with his parents. That was why, the one time when Saburō let slip a hint that he might follow his brothers and volunteer, Mr. Saeki could not hide his displeasure. He begged his son not to go. "You, at least, must stay with us."

As chief of the mess hall, Mr. Saeki used to be held in high esteem by the people of the block, both because of his quiet, gentlemanly demeanor and his standing as a devoted Christian. However, after his sons enlisted, everyone started to look at him askance. People who held contrary opinions attacked him for going soft. There were even some who, horrible as it is to say, called him a bootlicking lapdog. At the time, general sentiment in the camp was against enlisting, and he had sent not one but two of his sons to the army. Despite the rumors spreading behind his back, as far as Mr. Saeki was concerned, people who lived in America but did not respect America's laws or cooperate with her policies were no better than opportunistic parasites. So when people in camp called him a sissy, or a dog, he did not really mind. What bothered him was how people he worked with started to act strangely around him, or how people in block meetings would go out of their way to pretend he was not there. As the days passed, and people of the block kept their distance, shunning him as if he had already drifted away to some far-off land, he could not help but feel utterly alone.

There was no way that he could spend the rest of his life in camp like this. Mr. Saeki was already a complete outcast, and things were only getting more difficult. He realized that it was only a matter of time before he would have to leave, so he thought it best to try to get out sooner rather than later. He discussed the matter with his wife and Saburō, and since they were all in agreement, Mr. Saeki went straight to the office and completed the forms to apply for work outside of camp.

Several days later, the matter of his employment had been

settled and the family received permission to leave. The moment they got the news, the Saekis started to prepare for their promised date of departure. They got rid of things like their makeshift furniture and their old clothes, things that were good enough in camp, but that would be cause for embarrassment on the outside. As they cheerfully went about these preparations, and just when they were about ready to go, they received word that Saburō, the son he had asked to stay, was being drafted.

Even after he had sent two of his sons to the army, they were going to take Saburō, his youngest, the one he had hoped to rely upon. Mr. Saeki fell into despair. He used to be the kind of person who would make little jokes just to see his wife and the neighbors laugh. No longer. Every day he would walk around, despondent, looking so frail that his trailing figure seemed like a shadow about to disappear.

His wife would kneel in prayer every day with tears in her eyes. Seeing his wife's sadness, Mr. Saeki wished he could tell her how he truly felt so that they could share their sorrows. Instead, he tried to comfort her, and also himself, by saying, "Even if they've become soldiers, that doesn't mean they'll be deployed to the front lines, and even if that happens, that doesn't mean they're going to die." Then, with the devotion of a truly religious man, he would pray to God and do his best to forget his anguish.

There were some kindhearted people in the block who saw the sorrow of the Saekis, looked on them with sympathy, and tried to comfort them. But there were others who thought the Saekis were only reaping what they had sown, so took delight in their misfortunes, and cursed them. It was in this mixed atmosphere that the Saekis left behind many difficult memories, and out of which, in sadness, they departed.

* * *

Mr. Saeki had seventeen years of experience as a live-in cook, so his new employers were quite pleased with him. They also looked sympathetically upon the fact that he had sent three sons to the army, and it did not hurt that his former employer, a military man, had provided a recommendation that sang his praises. Life on the outside was worlds apart from all the criticism and misery that the Saekis had experienced in camp. After a few months, they were in brighter spirits and agreed that relocating had been the right decision.

Their sons would send them letters from afar, and the Saekis read them as if they were food for the starving. Relieved to hear that their sons were doing well, they prayed for their continued health and safety.

One day, the Saekis received a single envelope with letters from all three of their sons. Alarmed, Mr. Saeki opened the envelope to find that the two oldest had completed their combat training and were going to be sent to the front. The last letter was from Saburō. He wrote that, in all likelihood, he would be sent to the front line as soon as his training was over. Mr. Saeki felt as if he had been punched in the chest. His wife, who had been listening as he read the letters aloud, clasped her hands and prayed, her voice trembling as she wept. Ominous thoughts started to crowd Mr. Saeki's mind. He tried to brush them aside, but they would not leave.

After receiving these letters, Mr. Saeki seemed so utterly diminished that his employer thought that he might be going senile. The employers announced that they would throw a party to offer comfort to the Saekis and wish for the continued good fortune of their sons on the front lines. On the night of the party, the Saekis were seated as the guests of honor, surrounded by their employers' closest friends. There were only ten people, including the family, so it was a quiet event. To comfort the Saekis, the guests, all of them white, offered kind and heartfelt words of sympathy. In all of Mr. Saeki's many years, he had never been so moved to tears. He was so grateful for the kindness of his employers—a kindness that transcended ideas of race—and for these white people's expressions of goodwill. As the party was nearing its end, Mr. Saeki, flushed from the wine, stepped onto the balcony to catch the evening breeze.

Before his eyes lay the expanse of Lake Michigan, closed in darkness save for the flickering of streetlamps reflected upon its quiet surface. He loved this vista of Lake Michigan at night, seeing it as symbolic of America itself. The trees along the shoreline cast thin, trailing shadows into the lake as the moon made a sudden appearance, flashing whole on the surface of the water as if it had dropped, unchanged, from the sky. Every now and then a boat would ply its oars silently through the moon, splitting it in two perfect halves before drifting back into the shadows of the tree-lined shore. Then the noise of the city floated across the lake, breaking Mr. Saeki's quiet reverie. As he smoked his cigarette, he thought about the kind words of the partygoers. Even if they were just a temporary comfort, that was fine. As far as he was concerned, those words were cut straight from the heart, and he would think of them as real and true.

It was all for America, a country that held vistas of magnificent beauty like Lake Michigan. It was for the defense of democracy, for freedom, that his sons were risking their lives on the battlefield. They were sacrificing themselves to fight for their people, for the elimination of racial prejudice. Those were the things that his employers and their friends had said to comfort him. It was not as if Mr. Saeki felt that these words carried much meaning, but so long as it was for America, the country where he had decided to spend the last years of his life, then the sacrifices he had made so far were nothing special. All he had done was to raise his three sons to be loyal citizens of the United States, and for that alone those white people felt he was worthy of praise.

Three months passed, and it was on a rainy day, shortly after they had received the news that Saburō was being sent to the front lines, that they heard from Masuo. Jōji had been killed in action. Like being shot by a pistol, that was the shock Mr. Saeki felt in his chest, but he did not feel grief. Instead, his spirits were still buoyed by all the excitement from three months earlier. From the depths of their hearts, the Saekis prayed for Jōji, lost to the misfortunes of war. They made do with a perfunctory funeral.

Two weeks later, the Saekis made use of their day off to go downtown and buy thank-you gifts for friends in camp who had sent funeral offerings. Since Mr. Saeki disliked crowds, he rarely went shopping on his own, and it had been who knows how many years since the Saekis had gone shopping together. They did their best to find items that were not too extravagant, and it was evening by the time they returned. As they entered their room, they saw that someone from the household had placed a letter on the table. When Mr. Saeki realized that the sender was the Department of War, a chill ran up his spine. He was so terrified that at first he could not bring himself to open it. When he finally did, the letter read that Masuo had died a heroic death in Italy. Mrs. Saeki was standing next to him, her face drawn in worry, and when he told her that Masuo had died, she collapsed to the floor, let out an anguished cry, and wept. Mr. Saeki stood in total silence, as if lost in a daze, his hand still clutching the letter. All of the grief that he had been trying to suppress finally broke through the surface, and in that moment he felt like he wanted to burst into tears. He fell to his knees to shelter, and console, his crying wife.

The dreadful premonitions that Mr. Saeki had hoped would never, ever come to pass were happening, appearing right in front of him exactly as he had feared. When he stopped to think about this, he could not help but wonder if the war was somehow eerily capable of sensing and fulfilling his worst fears. And then worries about Saburō being sent to the front started to crowd his thoughts. What if something happened to Saburō . . . ? No, never . . . but Masuo and Jōji had both died, so chances were that he would die too. Mr. Saeki tried his best to stop these thoughts from floating up, but the more he tried, the more they surfaced, and his mind became flooded by ominous visions.

Not a day had gone by when Mr. Saeki had not longed for his home in Japan, but for the sake of the children's happiness, the Saekis had decided to spend their remaining years in America. Now two of their children were dead, and Mr. Saeki no longer understood why they had made this decision in the first place. It would be a relief if, at the very least, nothing happened to Saburō, but even that could not be guaranteed. Mr. Saeki felt utterly alone in this land so far from heaven. Why should he keep on living if there was nothing left to look forward to? When he had these thoughts, Mr. Saeki's sorrows overflowed their banks, and tears streamed down his face, a sadness without end.

Whenever Mrs. Saeki thought about her sons' deaths, she would say through her tears, "We should have sent Masuo back to Japan. Don't you remember how much he wanted to go? You held out on giving him just a little bit of travel money, and now look what's happened."

Whenever he heard this from his wife, Mr. Saeki would recall how angry he had been when he argued with Masuo about going to Japan and fall into dark regret. When his wife blamed him for Masuo's death, he could not abide the feeling of being attacked. To pull himself out of his torment, he would turn around and take it out on her.

The employers tried to console him, but no matter how many heartfelt expressions and kind words of comfort were thrown at him, none had any effect. *They died for the nation, they died for freedom*—all those beautiful decorous phrases now seemed thoughtless and shallow. They made him feel nothing but contempt. He would have preferred sharper, faster, more honest words. Now, night after night, when Mr. Saeki was done with his work for the day, he would join his wife and pray to God. And after he was done with his prayers, he would try to distract himself from his desolation by taking a walk along the shore of Lake Michigan. Sometimes he would walk with his wife, but most of the time he walked alone.

The soft breezes of early fall would blow across the lake as he walked along the sad narrow path. Whenever someone happened to walk toward him, Mr. Saeki would deliberately veer off and head toward the shadows beneath the densely tangled trees. There were moments when the forlorn note of the lake ferry's steam whistle would echo in his ears. Mr. Saeki's walks were usually occupied by thoughts of his sons, of their deaths in distant battlefields, but for some strange reason, whenever he heard the steam whistle, he started to think about his hometown. And then the memories would come, one after another, of his childhood in that place he had left and lost so long ago.

The hills, the rivers, and the ocean—the beautiful scenery of his ancestral home on the shores of the Inland Sea. Things he had forgotten years ago now felt like they were rushing back all at once. Why did he ever decide to abandon his beautiful home? For the sake of his children's happiness . . . In the end, perhaps those were just empty words he used to delude himself. Were his children really happy in America? Did he fulfill his duty as a parent? Did he teach his children the truth? These endless reflections were like waves pulling, returning, then pulling again on the shores of Mr. Saeki's weary heart, the surging tide of a longing for home.

Mr. Saeki was utterly exhausted. His body was drained of spirit. He could no longer work as well as before. There were many times when he just stood in the kitchen, staring off into emptiness. The employer was worried and offered to throw another party, but Mr. Saeki turned him down. No part of him felt like having a party. His employer suggested that he go somewhere for a vacation. He would feel like a new man. Mr. Saeki turned down this offer too. He no longer wished to speak with anyone. He feared that he would be overcome by his present sadness. If he could, he would go someplace far removed from human habitation, with no company but his sorrows held tight and close. That was how he felt. There were even times when he no longer felt like speaking with his wife. If anything, her sadness was far greater than his. She would be in the middle of cleaning the house, and if she thought of her sons, she would not be able to control herself. She would rush back to her room and weep. Mr. Saeki hated seeing his wife like this. The sight of her would stir up his own feelings beyond what he could bear.

Every now and then they would get the letters Saburō sent from the front lines. Each time Mr. Saeki read one of these letters, he would regain some measure of lost hope and feel some strength return to his body. To some degree, the sorrow of his loneliness would fade. Saburō's letters only hinted at the hardships of battle. When his unit stopped for the night, he would look up at the starry sky, and the sound of insects chirping would make him think of better times in camp. When Mr.

Saeki read these words, he thought of how pitiful it was that since Saburō had no place to call home, he could only long for camp. Mr. Saeki tried his best to write replies in his clumsy English. His wife would sit by his side and tell him to write this or that. Writing these letters was Mr. Saeki's one remaining joy.

Four months passed. Spring had reached even the western mountains, and the employers had returned from their vacation on the Pacific coast. It happened in the afternoon at the end of a busy week. A newspaper reporter came to the house at the very moment Mr. Saeki received the War Department notice of Saburō's death in combat. Lost in grief, Mr. Saeki stood in front of the staff photographer.

Mr. Saeki felt as if everything had gone dark before his eyes. He felt like cursing all that was left in this world. *What have I done to deserve such misfortune? How can I bear the weight of these terrible sacrifices?* He felt like doubting the existence of the God he had believed in for so many years.

He envied his employers, who had three sons of draft age, but had not sent even one of them to the military. He could not help resenting the fact that each of them had professions that were exempted, by law, from service. Two were in munitions, the other in agriculture—so they were, at least ostensibly, doing some form of work, but what did they, as individuals, actually do? They probably had no idea what their companies were making or what their farms produced. They were likely the kind of men who spent their nights fooling around, going from club to club, woman to woman. Even though these were the people who, in a just world, should have been defending the country, standing on the front lines with rifles in their hands, they were doing the exact opposite. These people had treated him with cold contempt for years and then sent his sons to the front lines to die. How could this happen in an America that prided itself on freedom, brotherhood, and justice? His sons had fought and died for America with the purest of intentions. His sons had vanished with the dew of the battlefield, all just to thicken the foundations of these people's hedonism. There was no such thing as freedom or justice in

America. It was all about money. Money determined who lived and who died.

Mr. Saeki knew that these twisted thoughts were just reactions to grief. Nevertheless, they lightened the burden of his sorrow a little bit, so he allowed himself to think them.

His employer had extended him the kindness of allowing him to take the next day off, but in the morning, Mr. Saeki went down to the kitchen to at least get the coffee started. As the coffee was brewing, the employer entered with a smile on his face. He said nothing as he handed Mr. Saeki the newspaper. Printed in the paper was an article about his three sons' deaths accompanied by a four-by-six-inch portrait of Mr. Saeki. The article included his remarks, with this quote:

> "When I think about how my three sons have died for America, I think of how content they are now in Heaven. When I think this, I do not feel sadness, but rather a far greater feeling of honorable happiness."

These were the words that Mr. Saeki had said to the journalist the day before, but reading them now, he wanted to vomit. These people had cursed him and stomped on him, taken all that he treasured, stripped him and left him naked, and still he was trying to flatter them. He could no longer stand the sight of himself. In the back of his mind, he saw the triumphant, laughing faces of all the people in camp who had called him soft and weak. Those people's faces became the faces of everyone in camp, even his closest friends, his family. Everyone was laughing at him. Mr. Saeki, his blood boiling, wanted to defy them, to shout at them, to call them damned fools. But those words just turned back upon him, expressions of his own self-loathing. Why didn't he just bash his head in against the wall? He wanted to beat himself senseless. He looked at the picture of himself in the newspaper and saw a perfect specimen of village idiot. Like tongues of flame, a violent anger flickered, caught, and burst within him. Mr. Saeki did not care that his employer was standing next to him. He crushed the paper into a crumpled ball, slammed it down into the wastepaper basket in the corner, and then stomped on the basket, smashing it with all his might.

* * *

Two weeks later, the Saekis were no longer in the house. Whether the employer fired them or they left of their own accord, I do not know. Sometime after, a Mexican woman stood on the balcony, admiring the magnificent vista of Lake Michigan. All races are welcome to join America's inclusive embrace, to fall in love with her mysterious charms.

44

FUYO TANAGI AND THE
MOTHERS SOCIETY
OF MINIDOKA

PETITION TO
PRESIDENT ROOSEVELT

Hunt, Idaho
February 20, 1944

Franklin D. Roosevelt
Executive Mansion
Washington, D.C.

Dear President Roosevelt:
Please allow us to present another earnest petition in regards to the reclassification of American Citizens of Japanese ancestry.

We, the parents of citizens of Japanese ancestry, longed for America, land of the free and equal, left behind our familiar birthplace, and came a great distance to this country. And in this land of strange language and customs, struggling against innumerable obstacles, we attempted to gain a secure means of living. In time with the grace of God our children were born in this country, and we brought them up as splendid American citizens, who could be pointed to with pride. They in turn did not disappoint us in our hope and grew up to be American citizens no less loyal than any other American.

This, we believe, is demonstrated by the lack of law-breakers among them and the fact that in proportion, the number of Japanese-Americans to volunteer for the Armed Forces, at the time conscription was ordered, was far above other nationalities.

When war broke out, unfortunately, between America and Japan, each time a Nisei draftee or volunteer left for the Army all of his relatives and friends encouraged and spurred him on and sent him off. This fact, we believe, shows the stand of Nisei citizens and their parents toward the war.

However, on the Pacific Coast with the so-called "military necessity" as a reason the foundation of our life, the fruit of several decades of toil and suffering, was completely overturned; and first-generation aliens and even Nisei—who are American citizens—were forced to lead a life within barbed-wire fences. This treatment that they received was far worse than that accorded to German and Italian enemy aliens.

About the time of evacuation from the Coast, their draft classification was changed to 4-C. They were considered enemy aliens. The blow to their spirit, that they suffered at this time, was something that we could hardly bear to witness.

Again, Lt.-General DeWitt, Commanding Officer of the Western Defense Command, proclaimed in reference to them that "a Jap's a Jap"; and, using a baseless and vague argument, accused Niseis of being spies and saboteurs, thus adding fuel to the anti-Nisei feeling among the people on the Coast. However, to this day, two and a half years since the outbreak of the war, not a single case of sabotage by a Nisei has occurred on the Pacific Coast or even in Hawaii.

But unfortunately the American public does not listen to the truth, and it seems that the discrimination against them is becoming even more intense.

Even today, although they are American citizens, Niseis are not allowed free travel through the Coast. Even Japanese war veterans who risked their lives for the United States and participated in World War I are interned in relocation centers. Since they have begun to feel deep down inside of them that these restrictions of freedom directed at American citizens of Japanese ancestry could not be understood as merely for the purpose of protection; we, their mothers, advised them that, this being war time, they should submit to military orders, and endure whatever place they are given.

Among them were some who, desiring to improve the present discriminatory condition of citizens of Japanese ancestry, requested the modification of the Selective Service regulations, or took it upon themselves to volunteer for the Armed Forces and to attempt to show their real spirit. However, they too received discriminatory treatment, even within the military camps; and, contemplating the course to be followed by their juniors, they are in a state of constant anguish.

We understand that the purpose for which the United States is allowing tremendous sacrifices in fighting the war today is to establish "freedom and equality" throughout the world. When they, the Nisei, consider the purpose of this war and then think about the treatment they are receiving at present, they discover the existence of a great paradox. They are dejected, and now have lost their firm, unshakeable faith and spirit. To think of sending them in this condition to the front, we, as mothers, considering the past and the future, feel an extreme and unbearable anguish.

Our loving and judicious Mrs. Roosevelt,

Please, from the standpoint of love for humanity, understand the feeling of the small number of suffering mothers, and advise us on the course that we should take. In this connection we would like to have you please consider the suspension of the drafting of citizens of Japanese ancestry until they regain the confidence that they can demonstrate their loyalty to the United States from the bottom of their hearts as formerly. And we earnestly petition to be granted gracious words of advice and humbly await a reply from you.

Very respectfully yours,

Mothers Society

[The petition was sent to the president and to Eleanor Roosevelt, but only the First Lady replied, with an unsigned note to which her staff added an explanation. —eds.]

March 4, 1944

Dear Mrs. Tanagi:
I have the letter signed by you and other members of the Mothers Society of Minidoka of the Minidoka Relocation Center.

The opportunity to serve through Selective Service may be the one thing which will make this nation see that Americans of Japanese descent should be treated in every way in the future like Americans after the war is over. Bitterness will pass and our sense of justice will make us treat our loyal citizens fairly, no matter what their origin.

Very sincerely yours,

Dictated but Mrs. Roosevelt
had to leave before signing.

45

YOSHITO KUROMIYA

FAIR PLAY COMMITTEE

As I approached the mess hall building, I noticed the absence of the usual clatter of dishes, pots, and pans. There were neither the familiar shrieks of children nor the incessant chatter of gossip. Also missing was the pungent aroma of steaming rice, homemade *takuan* (pickled daikon radish), and not-so-fresh fish, which would normally escape every time someone opened a door to enter or leave. There was only the deep rumbling of subdued voices, interrupted occasionally by the squeal of a table or bench dragging on the concrete floor. I entered the smoke-filled room, searching for familiar faces. Not finding any, I settled into an open space between two strangers on a hard wooden bench near the back of the room. I noticed my glasses didn't fog up as they usually did when entering the steamy mess hall on cold evenings. All the important players were sitting at two ten-foot-long tables abutted end to end at the front of the room where the serving counter acted as a barrier between the kitchen and the larger dining area. Papers were being shuffled back and forth among those at the front table. Sitting so far back and with all the smoke in the room, I couldn't see very well but I didn't mind. I was there primarily to hear, not see. Besides, close access to the rear door was reassuring in case I didn't like what I was to hear.

Suddenly, a middle-aged man (everyone seems to be middle-aged or elderly when you're twenty), rather slight of build, but with a voice of one twice his size, stood and announced in no uncertain terms the start of the meeting. This put an abrupt and permanent end to many unfinished sentences in the now-crowded room. Perhaps I exaggerate a bit in describing Kiyoshi Okamoto, but he was so atypical of the quiet, contained Japanese image. I was immediately captivated by his demeanor, directness, and (I hoped) his sincerity. His language was brutally crude, sprinkled generously with four-letter expletives, but the content was essentially an articulation of my own deeper thoughts and feelings. Further, he seemed to have an impressive knowledge of constitutional law, indispensable in any civil-rights forum. Other speakers followed, but I don't recall much of what was said. I was busy in my own head, separating the seed from the chaff, wondering if I had heard correctly.

I attended other meetings. I paid a two-dollar fee and was placed on the growing membership roster. The meetings were held in various mess halls whose managers were amenable to our cause (not all were). Each time I sat a little closer to the front table. I grew to respect all the male leaders (the steering committee) as principled individuals who knowingly jeopardized their own and their families' welfare in an effort to regain dignity, if not justice, for all inmates. Most were too old for the draft or had dependents, which would get them easy deferments. One (Guntaro Kubota) wasn't even a U.S. citizen, but he was concerned about the plight of those who were.

On about March 16, 1944, I received my notice to report for a physical exam prior to induction. Many thoughts ran through my head. I regarded the notice as yet another insult, the first being the curfew which now seemed so long ago. How could I continue to go along with this morally corrupt charade? I was being asked not to serve in defense of my country, but in a war of aggression in foreign lands for principles I was denied here at home. Further, it was presented as an opportunity to "prove my loyalty." Apparently, my guilt of disloyalty was assumed and I should welcome this opportunity to prove otherwise. Something was seriously amiss.

What of my family, still detained in this infernal prison

camp? What of our suspended constitutional rights? What of our past cooperation with the government in surrendering those rights in the name of "national security"? What of the democratic principles which had been denied us—the very principles we were now asked to defend on foreign soil?

NO! This is *my* country! This is *my* Constitution! This is *my* Bill of Rights! I am here finally to defend them. I regret that I had surrendered my freedom. I shall not continue to surrender my dignity nor the dignity of the U.S. Constitution!

Thus, after receiving the notice to report for the pre-induction exams, *I refused to comply!* Had the mainland United States been threatened with invasion, I would not have taken this stand. But to join in the killing and maiming in foreign lands, not because they were the enemy, but in order to prove my loyalty to a government that imprisoned me and my family without hearings or charges, I felt would be self-serving, irresponsible, and totally without conscience. Indeed, the real threat to our democracy was at my very doorstep.

At the next FPC meeting I sat at a front table, next to that of the steering committee. It was at a previous meeting that it was suggested there had been enough rhetoric and it was time to take a stand. The vote was almost unanimous, that a test case be initiated to determine the status of our citizenship and clarify our rights and obligations. The group had escalated from a passive protest forum to one of active resistance. The crowd at this point was well over the fire-restriction capacity for the building, perhaps by as much as 50 percent. They were mostly young Nisei men with a scattering of Issei parents and a few women of both generations.

In the course of the meeting they called for a show of hands of those who had received their pre-induction notices since the last meeting. Several, perhaps a dozen including myself, raised our hands. They asked me, perhaps because I was at the closest table, what I intended to do about it. I stood up and explained I was instructed to be on the bus to Powell on the morning of the twenty-third. Then I found myself declaring I would *not* be on that bus. There was a sudden cheer that rattled the windows and startled me. I felt a million eyes on me, and as exhilarating as it was, my knees began to buckle. I was thankful to sit down. There were others who stood and declared their intent to resist, but also a few who had not decided. I wondered how many who had received their notices were reluctant to even raise their hands.

As for me, I had passed the point of no return. It was now cast in stone. There would be no turning back.

46.

FRANK EMI AND
THE FAIR PLAY
COMMITTEE

WE HEREBY REFUSE
... IN ORDER TO
CONTEST THE ISSUE

FAIR PLAY COMMITTEE
"one for all—all for one"

"No person shall be deprived of life, liberty, or property, without due process of law, nor private property be taken for public use without just compensation."

Article V Bill of Rights

"Neither slavery nor <u>involuntary servitude</u>, except as punishment for crime whereof the party shall have been <u>duly convicted</u>, shall exist within the United States, or any place subject to their jurisdiction."

Article XIII Bill of Rights

We, the Nisei have been complacent and too inarticulate to the unconstitutional acts that we were subjected to. If ever there was a time or cause for decisive action, IT IS NOW!

We, the members of the FPC are not afraid to go to war—we are not afraid to risk our lives for our country. We would gladly sacrifice our lives to protect and uphold the principles and ideals of our country as set forth in the Constitution and the Bill of Rights, for on its inviolability depends the freedom, liberty, justice, and protection of all people including Japanese Americans and all other minority groups. But have we been given such freedom, such liberty, such justice, such protection? NO!! Without any hearings, without due process of law as guaranteed by the Constitution and Bill of Rights, without any charges filed against us, without any evidence of wrong-doing on our part, one hundred and ten thousand innocent people were kicked out of their homes, literally uprooted from where they have lived for the greater part of their life, and herded like dangerous criminals into concentration camps with barbed wire fences and military police guarding it, AND THEN, WITHOUT RECTIFICATION OF THE INJUS-TICES COMMITTED AGAINST US NOR WITHOUT RESTORATION OF OUR RIGHTS AS GUARANTEED BY THE CONSTITUTION, WE ARE ORDERED TO JOIN THE ARMY THRU DISCRIMINATORY PROCEDURES INTO A SEGREGATED COMBAT UNIT! Is that the Ameri-can way? NO! The FPC believes that unless such actions are opposed NOW, and steps taken to remedy such injustices and discriminations IMMEDIATELY, the future of all minorities and the future of this democratic nation is in danger.

Thus, the members of the FPC unanimously decided at their last open meeting that until we are restored all our rights, all discriminatory features of the Selective Service abolished, and measures are taken to remedy the past injustices thru Judicial pronouncement or Congressional act, we feel that the present program of drafting us from this concentration camp is unjust, unconstitutional, and against all principles of civilized usage. Therefore, WE MEMBERS OF THE FAIR PLAY COM-MITTEE HEREBY REFUSE TO GO TO THE PHYSICAL

<u>EXAMINATION OR TO THE INDUCTION</u> IF OR WHEN WE ARE CALLED IN ORDER TO <u>CONTEST THE ISSUE</u>.

We are not being disloyal. We are not evading the draft. We are all loyal Americans fighting for JUSTICE AND DEMOCRACY RIGHT HERE AT HOME. So, restore our rights as such, rectify the injustices of evacuation, of the concentration, of the detention, and of the pauperization as such. In short, treat us in accordance with the principles of the Constitution.

If what we are voicing is wrong, if what we ask is disloyal, if what we think is unpatriotic, then Abraham Lincoln, one of our greatest American Presidents was also guilty as such, for he said, "If by the mere force of numbers a majority should deprive a minority on any Constitutional right, it might in a moral point of view justify a revolution."

Among the one thousand odd members of the Fair Play Committee, there are Nisei men over the draft age and Nisei girls who are not directly affected by the present Selective Service program, but who believe in the ideals and principles of our country, therefore are helping the FPC in our fight against injustice and discriminations.

We hope that all persons whose ideals and interests are with us will do all they can to help us. <u>We may have to engage in court actions but as such actions require large sums of money, we do need financial support and when the time comes we hope that you will back us up to the limit</u>.

ATTENTION MEMBERS! FAIR PLAY COMMITTEE MEETING SUNDAY, MARCH 5, 2:00 P.M. BLOCK 6-30 MESS. PARENTS, BROTHERS, SISTERS, AND FRIENDS INVITED.

47

EDDIE YANAGISAKO AND KENROKU SUMIDA

SONG OF CHEYENNE

Translated by Violet Kazue de Cristoforo

Aloha, Cheyenne—inside the cage
Finally, seven men are living here,
Whiskers are shaggy—
Who has the longest?

Aloha, Laramie County, Wyoming.
Eight o'clock in the morning—at night, rumbling,
Poker games and gambling Hana cards.
Before sleeping—foolish talk.

Aloha, Heart Mountain. I long for you.
Don't know when I'll be back.
Pork sausage from mess hall
Caused diarrhea—running.

Aloha, Heart Mountain, I love thy sky.

Resegregation and Renunciation

AN ACT
To provide for loss of United States nationality
under certain circumstances.

Be it enacted by the Senate and House of Representatives of the United States of America in Congress assembled, That section 401 of the Nationality Act of 1940 (54 Stat. 1168; 8 U. S. C. 801) is amended by . . . adding a new subsection to be known as subsection (i) and to read as follows:

"(i) Making in the United States a formal written renunciation of nationality in such form as may be prescribed by, and before such officer as may be designated by, the Attorney General, whenever the United States shall be in a state of war and the Attorney General shall approve such renunciation as not contrary to the interests of national defense." . . .

Approved July 1, 1944.

48

NOBORU SHIRAI

WA SHOI WA SHOI, THE EMERGENCE OF THE "HEADBAND" GROUP

Translated by Ray Hosoda

According to our English language newsletter, the *Newell Star*, Congress had passed a bill on July 13, 1944, giving petitioners the right to renounce their citizenship despite the ongoing war. President Roosevelt promptly signed the bill. This gave new hope to a group of internees who wanted to return to Japan. Expecting to be shipped back to Japan as soon as possible, the resegregation and repatriation groups launched a resegregation movement.

A right-wing priest from Hawaii named Tsuha organized the Fatherland Study Youth Group (*Sokoku Kenkyu Seinendan*) to prepare the Nisei for life in Japan. Recruits had to pledge to (1) avoid involvement in the political struggles in the camp, (2) dedicate themselves to the study of Japanese culture and tradition, and (3) serve the fatherland upon arrival in Japan. Tsuha conducted an inaugural ceremony for the "Fatherland's Study Youth Group" in the Tule Lake Camp High School auditorium.

The leaders of the resegregation and repatriation groups thought that in order to become "true Japanese," young people must not only reject their U.S. citizenship, but also refuse an American education. They asked students to quit the public schools and enroll in either the Peoples' School (*Kokumin Gakko*) or the Greater East Asia Juku. These schools were approved by the movement's leaders.

There were strict dress codes for the members of the study group. The boys had to crop their hair close to their heads and wear gray sweatshirts as a uniform. The girls had to part their hair in the middle and braid it into two pigtails that reached the front of their shoulders. Later both boys and girls wore Rising Sun (*Hinomaru*) headbands. Because of this, the group was nicknamed either "the headband group" or the "short-cropped group."

In order to commemorate the day the U.S. declared war against Japan, December 8th, 1,200 members of the "Fatherland Service Group" (formerly the "Fatherland Study Youth Group") gathered in the plaza at 5 o'clock in the morning. The leaders had purified their bodies with cold water before coming to the plaza. In the predawn darkness, the crowd faced the direction of the Imperial Palace and prayed for Japan's victory. They worshiped the Emperor and then executed the gallant "National Exercise." After that, the whole group formed a column four abreast and fast marched around the compound in step with a bugle accompaniment. As they marched they chanted "*wa shoi, wa shoi.*" From that day on, the group assembled each morning for their military exercise.

Most of us were still sound asleep at 5 o'clock in the morning. We were annoyed to be awakened by the yelling, "*wa shoi, wa shoi*" and the blaring of the bugle. In my family, children usually awoke first. Once the children were up, my wife got up. When disturbed, it was difficult to go back to sleep. We could not recover from our lack of sleep and were irritable the rest of the day. For us, the ceremony before dawn was an annoying nuisance.

On one occasion, a 60-year-old woman with an "ain't gonna let the kids outdo me" attitude became very ill *wa shoi*-ing with the headband group. She kept up with the fast pace shouting "*wa shoi, wa shoi*," but she exhausted herself. It was a snowy day, and she was inadequately dressed in *mompe* pants. By that evening, she was running a high fever and had to be carried to the hospital. Her doctor diagnosed her as having acute pneumonia and ordered absolute bed rest. Needless to say, she was reprimanded for her participation in the outing.

The Fatherland Study Youth Group began with our blessings. We saw no harm in their motto, "Never meddle in camp politics," and encouraged their zest for studying Japanese culture. We also thought it was good for the young people to discipline themselves through physical training.

Our attitude changed as the membership of the group increased and they began to test their power. In the beginning, a priest headed the Fatherland Study Youth Group. Before we knew it, he was ousted and replaced by a man with a history of violence. The group was renamed the Fatherland Service Group (*Hokoku Hoshi-dan*), but behaved more like a terrorist organization. This group soon rivaled Kai and Kuratomi for influence in the camp.

Like the other activists, the Fatherland Service Group members also agitated for their causes and pressured people to cooperate with them. They extorted signatures for their petition to the Spanish Consul demanding their immediate return to Japan. Some members even assaulted the elderly on their way back from worshiping at the temple for refusing to sign.

There was a knifing incident in block 78 where the Fatherland Service Group was based. One of the detractors from the group got his face slashed. Fearing retaliation, he never notified the police or spoke out in protest. All he could do was cry himself to sleep, so to speak.

49

MOTOMU AKASHI

BADGES OF HONOR

Following the inauguration ceremony of the *Sokoku Kenkyu Seinen Dan* on August 13, 1944, my father took Tosh and me to meet Reverend Tsuha at Apartment 906-A2. The Reverend appeared to be a well-educated and well-read man, as evidenced by his large collection of books lined up on his apartment shelves. My father told us that Reverend Tsuha was a very important man and the principal organizer of the *Sokoku Dan* and that we should bow to him with respect, which, of course we did. My father then enrolled us as junior members of the *Sokoku Dan*. The age limit was sixteen. I was only fifteen, but an exception was made. Reverend Tsuha ceremoniously presented each of us with a gray sweatshirt emblazoned with the rising sun emblem, which was approximately 3" x 4" in size and located on the upper left side of the sweatshirt. He also presented us with a white *hachimaki* (headband), stenciled with a red round circle representing Japan. These were our "uniforms." He then instructed us to commit ourselves to being true Japanese, to wear these items as badges of honor and not to bring shame to the organization. He assigned us to the Ward 7 Branch and told us to report to Mr. Hoshinaga at 7216-C for further instructions.

We met Mr. Hoshinaga the next day, and he gave us an enthusiastic briefing on the purpose and goals of the *Sokoku Dan* and told us that we must train our body and mind with all our might to prepare ourselves for our future life in Japan. He said that by learning the Japanese culture and language and by physically building our bodies up through military exercises and drills we could become true Japanese. He told us to report to the assembly area that was the firebreak next to Block 72 at 5:30 a.m. the next morning. He said that he would introduce us to our platoon leader at that time. It was mandatory to cut our hair *bozu* (a shaved head) and wear the group's sweatshirt and headband. Absences would not be tolerated.

As directed, I had my hair cut *bozu*, a supreme sacrifice at that time. I had a beautiful thick lock of black hair and carefully combed it every day. I could not see myself as a "shave-head," but this was one of the rules for membership, so I complied.

The next morning, Tosh and I got up early, hurriedly dressed, put on our sweatshirts and headbands, and reported to Mr. Hoshinaga, who then introduced us to Mr. Ichizaka, our Block 74 platoon leader, who from that day on led us in Japanese military drills and calisthenics. As the sun rose, we stood at attention, faced west towards the Emperor's Palace and bowed in respect to the Emperor.

We practiced our military drills every morning and became quite proficient. Our platoon marched with pride in perfect precision. After the calisthenics, we joined with other platoons to form a company. Our company then joined with several other companies and together we ran around the perimeter of Ward 7, shouting "*washoi, washoi*" (cadence). The exercises built up our stamina and strength. I felt good. It was exciting and challenging. I enjoyed the sense of belonging and the camaraderie developed among other young members. This relationship of togetherness extended to our other activities during the course of the day. We went to school together and played sports together. We formed our own team and competed with other teams who were junior members of the organization.

For the first time, I felt good about being Japanese, not in a political or loyalty sense but being part of the Japanese race. I was not taunted, harassed or treated as a second-class citizen. I could hold my head up high and be treated as an equal. I did not feel that I had to subordinate myself, feel inferior or show deference to the whites as I often and subconsciously did when I was in Mt. Eden. I felt proud to be Japanese.

Soon after becoming a junior member of the *Sokoku Dan*, one of the leaders, Mr. Tanaka, asked for volunteers for the newly formed bugle corps. Of course, everyone wanted to be a bugler. I volunteered and was fortunate to be selected among twenty other volunteers. We were told to report to Mr. Muneaki for bugle training. In a solemn initiation ceremony, Mr. Muneaki issued us bugles that were purchased through Sears Roebuck. He impressed on us the honor of being selected and told us to treasure the bugle as a "badge of honor." He then taught us how to place our lips on the cup-shaped mouthpiece, tighten our lips, and blow so that our lips would vibrate and produce a sound. It was difficult at first, but eventually we got the knack of it and were able to produce harmonic sounds of the basic scale. Gradually, we became quite proficient and learned to play *Kimigayo* (the Japanese anthem) and a number of military calls and Japanese Army marching songs.

There was an open space directly east of Block 74, beyond the baseball field, where an armed guard on top of a watchtower overlooked the area. After school, I would go out there to practice. One day, a guard became irritated and shouted, "Hey, cut out that noise, you Jap boy." I ignored him and continued to practice. This time, the guard with an angry booming voice shouted, "I told you, Tojo boy, cut that out or I'll shoot you." I looked up and gave him the "finger." I defied him and in my youthful arrogance and ignorance, I confronted him with a gesture that would infuriate any red-blooded American. As luck would have it, the guard gave me another warning, this time louder and with much more authority, "You little twerp shithead, get the hell out of there. Now! Fast!" I came to my senses and took off like a rabbit never to practice there again.

Concurrent with learning how to play the bugle, Mr. Muneaki separated the twenty buglers from the main group and gave us drill instructions every day for about a month. He would assemble us with the command "*atsumare!*" (assemble). Then he would go through a series of short-order drills, such as *"kiot-suke"* (attention), *"migimuke migi"* (right face), *"hidarimuke hidari"* (left face), *"mawari migi"* (about face), and so forth.

At first, we were individually drilled, then as a squad and finally as a group. Mr. Muneaki had a loud and clear command voice. I was told that he was a drill sergeant and trained Japanese recruits in the Japanese Army when he was younger. In addition, Mr. Muneaki taught us how to blow a number of Japanese military marching scores and basic bugle calls, such as "assemble," "dismiss," "alert" and "emergency." He constantly emphasized the special honor and importance of the bugle corps. He outlined our duties and responsibilities and said that we should be the first to gather for the early morning drills and exercises. I took my task seriously, practiced every day and became quite proficient. I got up at 5:30 in the morning so that I would not miss first assembly at 6:00 a.m. I wore my gray *Sokoku* sweatshirt, tied the headband tightly around my head and darted out in the cold to the assembly point. I was proud to be a bugle boy.

The bugle corps lined up to the right of the main body and went through our morning calisthenics in cadence: *"ichi, ni, ichi; ichi, ni, ni; ichi, ni, san; ichi, ni, shi"* (1,2,1; 1,2,2; 1,2,3; 1,2,4) and so on. After the calisthenics, the group totaling three to four hundred young men and boys began our morning run. The bugle group formed in front, blew the marching song and kept the pace. When the command "double-time" was given, we quickened our pace, kept in step and in line, shuffled our feet in half steps and rhythmically shouted *"washoi, washoi, washoi."* We kept this up, running around the ward perimeter. It was an impressive display of unity, spirit and discipline. The morning ritual to the outsiders was annoying and a nuisance. They complained to the authorities that the *washoi* boys must be stopped. To us it was gratifying and gave meaning to being Japanese. . . .

On or about June 4, 1945, just before my sixteenth birthday as I recall, Mr. Muneaki announced that five of our buglers were charged with violating the new regulations that prohibited bugling and wearing the *Hokoku Dan* sweatshirt and headband. They were sentenced to the stockade for terms ranging from 120 to 370 days. They were teenagers, ranging in age from fifteen to seventeen. They were no older than I was. It could have easily been me.

Shortly thereafter, the bugle corps was disbanded. I felt lost and saddened without the early morning exercises, drills and marching. I had to get rid of my precious bugle, my headband and my sweatshirt. My spirits were low and demoralized. I really missed the pageant and ceremonies. There was nothing more exciting than to march six abreast in a formation of 300 to 500 men and boys, merging with other wards, and staging in one place over 10,000 people, sounding our bugles, marching in cadence and singing patriotic songs. It was exciting. I really enjoyed it. Now it was all gone. The authorities took away everything dear to me: first, my freedom, and then my bugle, headband and sweatshirt. All were my badges of honor.

50

JOE KURIHARA

JAPS THEY ARE,
CITIZENS OR NOT

1

They've kicked and cussed and on us spat
Calling us Japs, "the stabbers in the back"
Saboteurs and spies, these damnable Japs
Throw them into camps and ship them back.

2

In shameful words they forced us out
Into a desert like a bunch of sheep
They stole our homes and blasted our rights
With merciless sweep they broke us all.

3

For months and months we worked like slaves
"Take it or leave it" in pittance they've paid
Democracy they preach but practice not
Shaming tyranny, the frightful beast.

4

"Freedom of Speech" that's just in name
They've censored our mails; forbidden our speech
They threw us in jail for reason in want
Gestapo it was, in deeds and facts.

5

The food was sad, meager, and cheap
They gave us cows, tougher than hide
Beans! Beans! Beans! beans at noon and beans at night
Beans enough to feed the starving world.

6

The quarters were bare, small, and crude
Just walls with a roof and windows to boot
We sat on the bed, and wrote on our laps
The hell of a life we're made to like.

7

In midst of hate we've learned to smile
In silence we've borne their cowardly act
Humbly we follow, beastly they command
Greater they abuse to taunt our pride.

8

They've called us Japs; they've called us rats
They've called us names to ease their shame
They've killed our boys like dogs and cats
They've winked and jabbed in their court de sham.

9

Goodbye, America, Goodbye!
Jap I was born and as Jap I shall live
Proud as a cock to the world I crow
Jap I am and as Jap I will die!

51

HIROSHI KASHIWAGI

STARTING FROM LOOMIS . . . AGAIN

I renounced my American citizenship at Tule Lake, and I feel that was the dumbest thing I ever did in my life. It was a terrible mistake for I have paid dearly.

I had opposed the registration in protest against the many injustices suffered—not just the incarceration but all the racist abuses I had as a child and as a young man, all the times I had been called a "Jap."

For my action, or inaction, I was later segregated from the rest of the population. Me, a kid from Loomis, segregated in a maximum security prison for "disloyal" Americans. I didn't know what my fate would be; I was hoping that nothing drastic would happen.

I just wanted to be who I was—a Japanese American, an American of Japanese descent, an American citizen. Since they would not release me, I had no choice but to sit out the war in camp.

Obviously, I was not pro-Japan, even if I could read and write Japanese; I was, in fact, more advanced in the Japanese language than those hastily trained at the military language school. With my language skill, I realize now that I could have been very useful to my country. I would have been trained at the military language school and would have served in the Military Intelligence Service, where many Kibei and Nisei served with honor. If only the country had been more fair and trusting.

But renunciation was another thing. First the US Congress passed a law making it easier for American citizens to renounce their citizenship. When I first heard about the law, I felt it was only for pro-Japan fanatics, certainly not for me. I had no real desire to go to Japan so I tried not to concern myself with it. But unknowingly, I was swept into the clamor, and I succumbed to the pressure—both outside and within my family.

In the year after the loyalty questionnaire, Tule Lake became an increasingly tense, hostile, and dangerous place. Around 8,000 people from other camps who had also either refused to answer or answered no to the loyalty questionnaire were brought to Tule Lake; soon, talk of renunciation was in the air.

Pro-Japan factions were pressuring others; some urged me to join their group, the Hoshi Dan, and told me that for my own sake I must renounce my US citizenship. Although I refused to join them, I was also afraid of defying them. The atmosphere in camp was menacing—there were stealing and beatings and killings. It was dangerous to even speak English during this time because we would be called "White Japs." I grew increasingly afraid that I might become a marked man if I didn't follow the crowd.

In Block 40, where we lived, there was also agitation for repatriation, which often broke out in open hostilities. People questioned each other about where they stood on the subject. As I was secretary to the block manager, many people came to me asking for help in acquiring and filling out the repatriation forms. I listened to their questions and fears, and they only deepened my own.

I was influenced by a family friend whose wife and children were in Japan. He was planning to join them after the war, so it was natural for him to be pro-Japan. He came every day to visit Mother and to give us counsel, urging us to renounce. I tried not to listen to him, but I guess he was an influence—he was one of the few older male figures I could talk to. Though in my heart I didn't agree with him, I didn't want to defy him either.

My brother, who worked with some of the pro-Japan fanatics in the mess hall and came under their sway, forced the issue one day: "Are we American or are we Japanese? Let's make it clear." And I gave in.

In December 1944 I sent a letter requesting renunciation of citizenship for myself and my siblings. At the hearing in February 1945, I was afraid. I remember barely being able to speak. I had not talked with a Caucasian in over three years. Because of what had happened to us, I was filled with fear and distrust and resentment. We knew what questions would be asked from previous interviews; I just wanted to get it over with.

The renunciation was approved on March 22, 1945. I admit there was a brief feeling of relief once the ordeal was over. My mother was glad that, whatever might happen to us from then on, we would at least be together and be safe from the dangers inside and outside the camp. I also believed by that point that I was not wanted in America—my government had made that quite clear.

* * *

But renunciation was totally unnecessary. I realized that in the months to come, and I still believe it to this day. We had already made our protest known by not registering. Giving up our citizenship was stupid and redundant. Since I did not possess Japanese or any other citizenship, I essentially became a person without a country. My official status, in fact, became "Native American Alien"—what a preposterous predicament!

I think that after several years of incarceration I had lost all initiative to do anything new or daring on my own; I was barely hanging on, sticking to the familiar daily routine of camp life in fear that I would fall apart. Playing baseball with others like myself helped while we were involved in the game, but when the game ended it was back to bleak, numb reality. I guess this is what it is like to be incarcerated except that, in my case, my future was a big unknown—the war between the United States and Japan was still going on.

Still, I was lazy; I didn't want to think; I didn't want to confront the problem and make a decision, put my foot down, and assert my real feelings. Without Father there to guide us, I had a responsibility, and I know now that I should have stood up to my younger brother. Honestly, I never relished being the *chonan*, the firstborn son, not since we were kids. My brother, who was always tough, a class leader if not a bully, liked to be in control; by the time we were sharecropping the farm, he was doing the heavy work. In addition, like his father, he always planned several days ahead so he was on top of things. So I let him be the chonan, and our roles were reversed. I was happy with that until renunciation—when he forced the issue of our citizenship and I felt that I gave in to his power play. I think I thought all of it would somehow go away. For my refusal to face reality, I would pay dearly.

Perhaps I should not be too hard on myself? Perhaps I was the victim? I feel I have paid many times over for the position I took at Tule Lake. Certainly, you don't go around telling people you spent time at Tule Lake and gave up your citizenship during the war. You try to push that back somewhere and not think about it; you try to block out that part of your life, but you have to live with it. You try to find a safe niche in society and hope no one will pry into your past. Living under such pressure, it's inevitable that there should be doubts and questions about your actions, as well as feelings of guilt. Were my actions wrong or bad? What kind of man did this make me? I guess I couldn't help but live with these feelings as the years went on and I grew older.

PART III

AFTER CAMP

For decades after the war, Japanese Americans upon introduction to each other politely ask, ". . . and what camp were you in?" as a way to locate that person and their particular journey. "After Camp" now covers a three-quarter-century span that has seen citizenship for the Issei, an awakening by the Nisei to seek justice, the growth of the Sansei to become elders themselves, and work by fourth- and fifth-generation descendants to connect with and understand the legacy of incarceration they've inherited.

RESETTLEMENT AND RECONNECTION

The mass dispersal upon the closing of the WRA camps is well underway at the time *Rohwer Outpost* columnist James "Bean" Takeda takes a satiric look at this last great migration in "The Year Is 2045," a work of speculative fiction with an eerily prescient prediction of white separatism. Resettlers pioneer new lives in the East and Midwest, while many of those returning to the West Coast have lost homes or farms and must start over. The incarceration costs the community a generation of accumulated wealth and advancement, at the same time that anti-Japanese leagues organize to scare away former residents from returning. Where the community was once optimistic, poet David Mura shows how "Internment Camp Psychology" has scarred their outlook. The racism is especially virulent at Hood River, Oregon, where Shizue Iwatsuki writes a series of *tanka* about "Returning Home" and signing papers under the Immigration Act of 1952 that grant her and other Issei their long-denied naturalized U.S. citizenship.

Whenever the subject of the camps is broached in public, the prevailing cry is to "Remember Pearl Harbor" and for Japanese Americans to shut up and be grateful for what is claimed to be their humane treatment in camps where they were fed and educated. Their Sansei children will resent their parents for never talking to them about camp, but throughout the 1950s and 1960s Japanese Americans have no viable language to understand what happened to them, no script to express the trauma of mass incarceration. Able to see themselves only as pawns of war or victims of history and circumstance, most former incarcerees prefer to forget and move on. Only a few writers try to unpack the truth of their experience, as Toyo Suyemoto does in revisiting the ruins of her former barracks home in the desert of "Topaz, Utah."

The only language for the Sansei to seize upon in the 1970s is that of the civil rights, ethnic studies, and Third World movements; in "We, the Dangerous," poet Janice Mirikitani defiantly links Tule Lake to the U.S. bombings of Asians at Hiroshima and in Vietnam. As time passes, the distance from the firsthand experience of camp requires those born after the war to connect the dots through scraps of family lore. Concrete details provide a point of entry. An aerial photograph of the barracks at Gila River links Amy Uyematsu with her mother's imprisonment there in "December 7 Always Brings Christmas Early." In "Your Hands Guide Me Through Trains," Brian Komei Dempster finds meaning in the wrinkles in the hands of his grandfather, who was among the Buddhist priests transported to a Justice Department internment camp, while for Christine Kitano it is her father's story about what he packed that sparks the poetic imagination in "1942: In Response to Executive Order 9066, My Father, Sixteen, Takes."

REDRESS

By the 1970s, with their children grown and pressing them with questions, the Nisei regain their voice. The postwar JACL adopts biennial resolutions that dare to say out loud that the camps were wrong and that the government needs to atone in some meaningful way. Shosuke Sasaki, a retired Issei securities analyst with the Seattle Evacuation Redress Committee, forges a language in 1975 for reframing the wartime experience with "An Appeal for Action to Obtain Redress for the World War II Evacuation and Imprisonment of Japanese Americans." Rather than dwelling on the massive losses of property and income then estimated in the billions of dollars, the Sasaki manifesto focuses on the loss of freedom and the damage done to the Constitution as the basis for redress.

To demonstrate popular support, the Seattle group stages the first-ever Day of Remembrance in 1978 to remember the camps and stand for redress with their families. Two thousand turn out for a car caravan from Seattle to the Puyallup fairgrounds, which encourages their congressman Mike Lowry to introduce a redress bill for individual reparations. The four Japanese American members then in Congress carve out a compromise through creation of the fact-finding Commission on Wartime Relocation and Internment of Civilians (CWRIC), which in 1981 holds twenty days of public hearings in ten cities. Within two years, the CWRIC issues its findings of fact and recommendations in a report written by special counsel Angus Macbeth: that the root cause of the exclusion was not military necessity, as claimed by General DeWitt, but a combination of race prejudice, war hysteria, and the failed leadership of President Roosevelt and the wartime Congress.

The commission recommends that the modern-day Congress enact redress, but former Manzanar incarceree William Hohri, impatient with the pace of legislation, recruits fellow plaintiffs to file a class-action lawsuit under the banner of the National Council for Japanese American Redress (NCJAR), with a "Complaint" that names twenty-two causes of action against the government. Around the same time, documents are discovered showing that the War Department suppressed evidence of Japanese American innocence from the Supreme Court in World War II, providing an opportunity for Sansei lawyers to reopen the cases of Fred Korematsu, Gordon Hirabayashi, and Min Yasui. Jeanne Sakata dramatizes their "*Coram Nobis* Press Conference" in her radio play, *For Us All*.

Taken together, these movements compel Congress to pass the Civil Liberties Act of 1988 and President Ronald Reagan to sign it, a remarkably quick turnaround from the first public demonstration just ten years before. The act provides $20,000 for individual compensation for the violation of constitutional protections of due process and equal protection under the law, but of equal value to many former incarcerees is their letter from the White House, which several frame on their wall saying that all they ever wanted was for the government to apologize. For the many who never live to see that day, however, justice delayed is justice denied, as traci kato-kiriyama mourns in "No Redress"; she is among those who have joined with African Americans to make the case for Black reparations.

REPEATING HISTORY

The same fears of the "other" that drove the wartime incarceration explode into view whenever America feels itself threatened from abroad. The imports of cars and consumer electronics from Japan in the 1980s stoke alarms of an "economic Pearl Harbor," culminating in the beating death of Vincent Chin by two Detroit autoworkers. Perry Miyake's novel, *21st Century Manzanar*, reimagines this anxiety as the fuel for a ReVac, or "Evacuation, the Sequel." The suicide terror attacks at the World Trade Center on September 11, 2001, provoke the racial profiling and threatened roundup of Muslims, Arab Americans, and anyone who looks like them, to which Fred Korematsu asks, "Do We Really Need to Relearn the Lessons of Japanese American Internment?"

The election of 2016 legitimizes racial division and latent white nationalism at the very top of the U.S. government, with a ban on travel from majority-Muslim nations, attempts to wall off the southern border, and the caging of asylum seekers from Latin America. "We Have Been Here Before," reports Brandon Shimoda after witnessing Japanese Americans standing as allies with families being separated at Fort Sill, Texas—the same former army internment camp where Otokichi Ozaki was once held with seven hundred other Issei and had his inmate number painted in red on his chest. Brynn Saito's "Theses on the Philosophy of History" captures the weariness of a people who must bear witness to this cycle of repeating events. Echoing the watchcry of "Never Again Is Now," the final pages of the graphic novel *We Hereby Refuse* bring us full circle from the *manga* of the first Issei.

In World War II, an American president singled out Japanese Americans for exclusion based solely on their race. Following a global pandemic, the lingering memory of an American president who invoked fear of a "China virus" and "kung flu" continues to legitimize violence against Asian Americans today. Political opportunists continue to target people on the margins on the basis of race, religion, immigration status, sexual orientation, or gender identity. Until the day that changes, the literature of Japanese American incarceration is one that will continue to be written.

Resettlement and Reconnection

52

JAMES TAKEDA

(as Bean Takeda)

THE YEAR IS 2045

The year is 2045, and the time is 6 o'clock in the evening. The season is late spring. The locale is Desha County, Arkansas.

Two figures emerge from the woods and stop at the edge of the clearing.

They are apparently human beings, but they look like creatures out of the prehistoric past. They are clothed only in loincloths and are barefooted.

One is a middle-aged man, of Japanese descent, about fifty, of medium height, fairly tanned, stockily-built, and covered with hair almost from head to foot.

The other is apparently his son, a lad of about 14, husky, with thick black hair on his head and a light covering of hirsute on his body.

The boy asks, "Pop, what are those broken-down shacks lined up in a row over there?"

"That, my boy, is what remains of Rohwer relocation center."

The boy was puzzled. "What was that, pop?"

"Well, my son, over a hundred years ago, at the outbreak of the Great War, all people of Japanese descent were evacuated from the West Coast and placed in centers. This was one of those centers, and over 12,000 people lived here at one time or another during the three years that it existed."

"Where did they all go, pop?"

"They scattered out, son. Relocation they called it. Some went east, others went north to places like Chicago, and others returned to California."

"Where is California, pop?"

"California, my son, is on the Pacific coast. It used to be one of our great states, until it withdrew from the union."

"Why did it withdraw, pop?"

"Because they wanted to keep it a white man's country, my son. Some of the people there didn't believe in liberty, equality, and democracy."

"Who were some of those people, pop?"

"Well, there were organizations like the California Preservation League and others with various names, but all formed for the same purpose. Then there was a man named John Lechner, who was born in Austria and who went around filling people's minds with lies and hatred."

"What happened to him, pop?"

"Oh, his mind became so warped that they locked him up in an insane asylum, and he died a raving maniac."

"Where did we come from, pop?"

"My son, we descended from the people who refused to leave the center here. They just stayed here, even after the center closed."

"Why did they refuse to leave, pop?"

"For various reasons, son. Some were afraid to leave, others liked it here, and still others refused to leave on general principles."

"How many of us descendants are there here, pop?"

"About 300 of us, son, scattered throughout the woods. There may be more on the other side of the river. But here, son, let's be getting home. It's getting late, and mother probably has fried tree roots for us tonight."

DAVID MURA

INTERNMENT CAMP
PSYCHOLOGY

circa 1945

Just after his release Mas took a psychological test.

Three questions he never forgot: Do you think

people are out to get you? Do you feel you are

being followed? When you see a crowd of strangers

walking toward you, do you try to avoid them?

To all three he answered yes.

And knew he sounded insane.

SHIZUE IWATSUKI

RETURNING HOME

Translated by Stephen W. Kohl

1. Going home,
   Gripping my daughter's hand,
   Feeling cheated,
   I tell her we're leaving
   Without emotion.

2. Through the car window
   A glimpse of pines.
   Oregon mountains.
   My heart beats faster,
   Returning home.

3. Four years have passed,
   Returning home
   Though I have no flowers to offer,
   First I visit my child's grave.

4. Evening twilight,
   Mother cow chews her cud.
   Beneath her
   The calf dozes.

5. Home at last
   At the dinner table

My husband calls my name,
But lapses into silence.
His heart, too, is full.

6. He was kind to us before,
   But now—the shopkeeper
   Nervously refuses to serve us.

7. Hard at work
   Rebuilding our life,
   To help my husband
   Today I go
   To buy farm tools.

8. Glancing up,
   At red-tinged mountains
   My heart is softened.
   A day in deep autumn.

9. Pointing out the trail to the summit
   He says it's steep,
   But we agree to try.

10. War and change,
    My native land
    Once so hard to leave,
    Is behind me now forever.

11. With determination
    I sign the naturalization papers.
    In my hand
    The pen trembles slightly.

12. A naturalized citizen now
    I have the right to vote.
    So today I climb
    The steps of this building.

TOYO SUYEMOTO

TOPAZ, UTAH

The desert must have claimed its own
Now that the wayfarers are gone,
And silence has replaced voices
Except for intermittent noises,
Like windy footsteps through the dust,
Or gliding of a snake that must
Escape the sun, or sage rustling.
Or soft brush of a quickened wing
Against the air. — Stillness is change
For this abandoned place, where strange
And foreign tongues had routed peace
Until the refugees' release
Restored calm to the wilderness,
And prairie dogs no longer fear
When shadows shift and disappear.
The crows fly straight through settling dusk,
The desert like an empty husk,
Holding the small swift sounds that run
To cover when the day is done.

JANICE MIRIKITANI

WE, THE DANGEROUS

I swore
it would not devour me
I swore
it would not humble me
I swore
it would not break me.

    And they commanded we dwell in the desert
    Our children be spawn of barbed wire and barracks

We, closer to the earth,
squat, short thighed,
knowing the dust better.

    And they would have us make the garden
    Rake the grass to soothe their feet

We, akin to the jungle,
plotting with the snake,
tails shedding in civilized America.

    And they would have us skin their fish
    deft hands like blades / sliding back flesh / bloodless

We, who awake in the river
Ocean's child
Whale eater.

And they would have us strange scented women,
Round shouldered / strong and yellow / like the moon
to pull the thread to the cloth
to loosen their backs massaged in myth

We, who fill the secret bed,
the sweat shops
the laundries.

And they would dress us in napalm,
Skin shred to clothe the earth,
Bodies filling pock marked fields.
Dead fish bloating our harbors.

We, the dangerous,
Dwelling in the ocean.
Akin to the jungle.
Close to the earth.

Hiroshima
Vietnam
Tule Lake

And yet we were not devoured.
And yet we were not humbled
And yet we are not broken.

57

AMY UYEMATSU

DECEMBER 7 ALWAYS BRINGS CHRISTMAS EARLY

All persons of Japanese ancestry, both alien and nonalien, will be evacuated from the above designated area by 12:00 noon.

—Executive Order 9066, Franklin D. Roosevelt, 1942

december 7 always brings christmas early
in neat white packages
red circles perfectly centered
one to a side

mama was taken away in a long railed box
blinds pulled taut to hold in her shame

they delivered her to a box in santa anita
walls lined with tissue paper hay
layered over manure and the bloody vomit
that gushes from caged animals

they confined her to a tarbacked box
in that flattened arizona desert
and in aerial photographs

the human cartons arranged row by row
framed by impeccably straight cornered wire borders
were picture perfect

they put me in an airless box
every december 7
when the history lesson was me
they gave me to babies
who were just learning the habits
of their fathers

forty years later the presents arrive
in one continuing commemoration
each precisely wrapped in black and white newsprint
houston st. louis new york
davis boston west philadelphia
in detroit the autoworker at the bar
didn't need to know the skull he smashed
belonged to vincent chin a name that didn't match

the evacuation of bodies resumes
judged by the same eyes that watched mama's train

58

BRIAN KOMEI DEMPSTER

YOUR HANDS GUIDE ME THROUGH TRAINS

From the bridge we stare down at the track, searching
the arch, where rails curve out of darkness. You lift me
on your shoulders and we balance in white light, the dead
    center
approaching. The whistle blows, a rumble climbs
through the bones of your feet, through your legs and hands
    into mine,

your right hand clenches my right,
your left hand clenches my left,
if this were 1942, my hands would be the handle
of your suitcase and your purple book scripted
in prayer. Torn from family, you board a boxcar, snap open

your case, set your brush and ink to the right,
stones to the left, paint your own sea and coast
as the plains, grass, and ironwoods rattle by.
You dip the brush in each camp and each barrack,
fill the paper with kelp and jellyfish, pebbles and shells,

tape the sheets side by side. When it grows
dark, you draw tracks leading to the edge of the tide.
Asking for water, your hands unclasp and cling

to the wires as men rip the sash from your back.
A rifle butt knocks prayer loose from your throat.

But it is 1976, a Sunday like any other,
when you drape beads over my wrists and open
the Lotus Sutra on the bridge, anchor its pages with stones,
offer prayers as the train rushes under our feet,
our lungs flowering with soot and steam.

For years, I traveled to your hands, unrolled ocean scrolls
from your case. In barracks you'd held the brush, painting
your way out. By 1996 your brushstrokes fade, *washi*
    crumples
in my palms. Your fingers grip a cane, waver with chopsticks.
Soup, tea, and rice sprig your bib. I feed you, brush your
    teeth,

my right hand clenches your right, my left clenches your left,
I lower you in the chair, place your feet on the steel ledges.
Grandfather, can we run just once through the gravel,
    along silver rail,
watch flames curl off the faces of men smudged in coal?
Can you take me to Missoula and Fort Sill, wheels circling
    back

to Crystal City? We arrive at the church where you live,
    and I wheel you
past rows of empty chairs, drape the sash over your back,
    strike
a match, light sticks of incense. Your hands guide me
through the years like a black iron rope, into the orange
    glow,
a tunnel of smoke, pages returning us to the shores of our
    home.

—*for Archbishop Nitten Ishida, 1901–1996*

59

CHRISTINE KITANO

1942: IN RESPONSE TO EXECUTIVE ORDER 9066, MY FATHER, SIXTEEN, TAKES

No spare underwear.
No clean shirts, pants, or good shoes.
Instead, a suitcase
of records. His trombone.
This is not the whole story,
and yet, it is true.
It is a story without an ending.
And when I open my mouth
to speak, it continues.

Redress

SHOSUKE SASAKI AND THE SEATTLE EVACUATION REDRESS COMMITTEE

AN APPEAL FOR ACTION TO OBTAIN REDRESS FOR THE WORLD WAR II EVACUATION AND IMPRISONMENT OF JAPANESE AMERICANS

Among the documents which form the philosophical and legal foundations of our nation, such as The Declaration of Independence and The Constitution of the United States of America, no idea is more basic in the origin and development of American history, traditions and statutes than the principle of equality of all persons before the law. Even the most cursory study of our nation's history leads to the inescapable conclusion that in the opinion of the Founding Fathers, such as Franklin, Adams and Jefferson, true Americanism meant an unbending insistence by each individual that any government accord him equality of treatment before its laws and refrain from unjustly violating certain "unalienable rights" such as "life, liberty and the pursuit of happiness."

Over thirty years ago, a few months after the entry of the United States into World War II, the Government of the United States without a shred of evidence of misconduct or disloyalty and without even a pretense of a trial, perpetrated the wholesale uprooting and imprisonment of practically all Pacific Coast residents of Japanese ancestry. True, the Government did not engage in systematic murder of Japanese Americans, but it did callously dispossess us of practically all the rest of our rights, such as the right to a fair trial, liberty, our jobs, our businesses, and our homes. This monstrous violation of the most basic of American traditions and laws relating to human freedom was the culmination of four decades of anti-Japanese propaganda of the most vile, outrageous and pervasive sort, particularly in the newspapers printed in the Pacific Coast states.

This propaganda brain-washed the mass of white Americans into feeling that the Japanese were subhuman creatures deserving of no rights whatever and brain-washed the Japanese Americans into thinking that they had been born of an unworthy race and that they had to submit meekly to practically any governmental trampling of their human rights in order to "prove" to others that the Nisei were "loyal Americans." The fact that, even after a lapse of thirty years, no real attempt has been made by Japanese Americans to obtain redress for the wrongs, humiliations and loss of income suffered by them during their totally unwarranted imprisonment indicates that the older Nisei at least, have been so psychologically crippled by their pre-war and wartime experience that they have been unable to act as Americans should.

Passive submission or self-abasement when confronted by government tyranny or injustice was alien to the beliefs held by the founders of this nation. If, in the face of British government tyranny, they had acted like the Nisei have in the face of American government tyranny, there would be no 200th Anniversary of the founding of our country to celebrate. In commemorating the birth of our nation, therefore, it is time that

Americans of Japanese ancestry repudiate the pseudo-American doctrine, promoted by white racists and apparently believed in by some former Nisei leaders, that there is one kind of Americanism for whites and another kind for non-whites. If Japanese Americans are as American as the J.A.C.L. has often claimed, then they should act like Americans and make every effort to seek redress through legislation and the courts for the rape of almost all their "unalienable rights" by the United States Government over thirty years ago.

Judging from the polls taken on the attitudes of the people living in the Pacific Northwest areas and the quantity of anti-Japanese hate mail and phone calls to local television stations immediately following programs dealing honestly with the evacuation and incarceration of Japanese Americans, over half of the white population of those areas believe to this day that the World War II treatment of the Japanese Americans was justified and that there was truth in the charges against us of espionage and sabotage.

By custom and tradition, any American who has been injured as a result of false accusations is expected to bring those responsible into court and obtain a judgment clearing his name and awarding him monetary damages from the offending parties. Failure by the slandered or libeled person to take legal action against his accusers is often regarded by the public as an indication that the charges are true. . . .

No amount of docile submission to white officials or "demonstrations of loyalty" to the United States by the Nisei can ever "disprove" the false accusations in the minds of most white Americans. That can only be done when the Government of the United States either through Congress or through its courts publicly declares that the wartime uprooting and imprisonment of Japanese Americans was totally without justification and awards the victims of its wartime outrage proper and reasonable redress. . . .

Except for approximately 10% of the Nisei who are convinced that they "have it made" or have been "accepted by the whites" and are opposed to any action which would "rock the boat," there is general agreement among Japanese Americans that action to obtain redress for the evacuation and related injustices is needed. Recent surveys show that a heavy majority want any payments made directly to each individual claimant. The surveys also reveal almost total agreement that the Issei should be given first priority in receiving such payments. . . .

In seeking redress, the nature of injuries and losses for which we hope to obtain monetary compensation must first be understood. Through the provisions of the Evacuation Claims Bill which was signed into law in 1948, former evacuees received (after legal and processing fees) a total net payment of $34,200,000 as "compensation" for their property losses which were estimated by the Federal Reserve Bank of San Francisco at $400,000,000 in 1942. Under the terms of those payments, we now are precluded from asking for a more just settlement for losses of property. Our present efforts, therefore, are directed toward obtaining redress for other injuries and losses.

For the mental and emotional suffering at the time of the evacuation and the psychological injuries sustained from the exile from their homes no fair compensation in dollars can be computed. Almost equally impossible would be any attempt to place a dollar value on the educational losses inflicted on the Japanese Americans of school age by the sudden termination of their normal schooling and by the Government's suppression of the teaching of the Japanese language and certain branches of Japanese culture. On the basis of recent court awards to persons subjected to unjustified imprisonment of even a few days, a payment of at least $5,000 to each person forced to leave his domicile as a result of the Evacuation Order in 1942 would appear to be appropriate. When the difficulties and costs to the evacuees in later settling in other areas of the country or in returning to their home areas on the Pacific Coast are also considered, the sum we suggest is far from excessive.

Furthermore, we believe that we are entitled to seek compensation from the Government for first, the prolonged loss of our personal liberty, second, for the loss of normal wage and salary incomes, and third, for the loss of business income for those who owned their businesses and farms. According to our estimates, based on 1942 dollars, the total wages and salaries lost by the Japanese Americans during their imprisonment was in excess of $400,000,000. No amounts for the value of lost pension rights, job seniority, lost opportunities for promotion, etc. are included in that figure. The total loss to Japanese Americans of the net incomes of businesses and farms which they were forced to leave behind as a result of their imprisonment is estimated by us to have amounted to over $200,000,000 in 1942 dollars. To cover these three classes of losses, we are suggesting a payment to each former inmate of those prison camps of $10 a day for each day of confinement, in addition to the flat payment of $5,000 already mentioned. . . .

Despite resolutions repeatedly passed at successive national J.A.C.L. conventions in favor of seeking reparations, a surprising succession of national officers and staff members have displayed a glacial reluctance to start any kind of effective moves toward such a goal. About their only contributions to discussions of the subject have been to emphasize the difficulties which would attend any such efforts. . . .

The members of the Seattle Chapter of the J.A.C.L. earnestly ask for the help and cooperation of your organization in these efforts, not only to obtain justice in the form of reparation payments to the innocent victims of the World War II evacuation and imprisonment, but also to have the Government of the United States thereby demonstrate to the whole world that it still has the greatness of spirit to acknowledge and provide redress for its past miscarriages of justice. Such Government action would prove conclusively that the concept of the equality of all persons before the law, as conceived by the Founding Fathers, continues to remain a fundamental principle of our nation. And, that The Constitution of the United States of America even 200 years after its birth cannot be permanently set aside and ignored by government officials no matter what rank or post they may occupy.

PREPARED BY THE EDITORIAL GROUP
Shosuke Sasaki, Editor

Mike Nakata
Henry J. Miyatake

EVACUATION REDRESS COMMITTEE,
SEATTLE JACL CHAPTER

APPROVED FOR DISTRIBUTION BY THE
SEATTLE JACL OFFICERS AND THE BOARD
OF DIRECTORS – November 19, 1975

In sum, Executive Order 9066 was not justified by military necessity, and the decisions that followed from it—exclusion, detention, the ending of detention and the ending of exclusion—were not founded upon military considerations. The broad historical causes that shaped these decisions were race prejudice, war hysteria and a failure of political leadership. Widespread ignorance about Americans of Japanese descent contributed to a policy conceived in haste and executed in an atmosphere of fear and anger at Japan. A grave personal injustice was done to the American citizens and resident aliens of Japanese ancestry who, without individual review or any probative evidence against them, were excluded, removed and detained by the United States during World War II.

The excluded people suffered enormous damages and losses, both material and intangible. To the disastrous loss of farms, businesses and homes must be added the disruption for many years of careers and professional lives, as well as the long-term loss of income, earnings and opportunity. Japanese American participation in the postwar boom was delayed and damaged by the losses of valuable land and growing enterprises on the West Coast which they sustained in 1942. An analysis of the economic losses suffered as a consequence of the exclusion and detention was performed for the Commission, Congress having extended the Commission's life in large measure to permit such a study. It is estimated that, as a result of the exclusion and detention, in 1945 dollars the ethnic Japanese lost between $108 and $164 million in income and between $41 and $206 million in property for which no compensation was made after the war under the terms of the Japanese-American Evacuation Claims Act. Adjusting these figures to account for inflation alone, the total losses of income and property fall between $810 million and $2 billion in 1983 dollars. It has not been possible to calculate the effects upon human capital of lost education, job training and the like.

Less tangibly, the ethnic Japanese suffered the injury of unjustified stigma that marked the excluded. There were physical illnesses and injuries directly related to detention, but the deprivation of liberty is no less injurious because it wounds the spirit rather than the body. Evacuation and relocation brought psychological pain, and the weakening of a traditionally strong family structure under pressure of separation and camp conditions. No price can be placed on these deprivations.

These facts present the Commission with a complex problem of great magnitude to which there is no ready or satisfactory answer. No amount of money can fully compensate the excluded people for their losses and sufferings. Two and a half years behind the barbed-wire of a relocation camp, branded potentially disloyal because of one's ethnicity alone—these injustices cannot neatly be translated into dollars and cents. Some find such an attempt in itself a means of minimizing the enormity of these events in a constitutional republic. History cannot be undone; anything we do now must inevitably be an expression of regret and an affirmation of our better values as a nation, not an accounting which balances or erases the events of the war. That is now beyond anyone's power.

It is well within our power, however, to provide remedies for violations of our own laws and principles. This is one important reason for the several forms of redress recommended below. Another is that our nation's ability to honor democratic values even in times of stress depends largely upon our collective memory of lapses from our constitutional commitment to liberty and due process. Nations that forget or ignore injustices are more likely to repeat them.

The governmental decisions of 1942 were not the work of a few men driven by animus, but decisions supported or accepted by public servants from nearly every part of the political spectrum. Nor did sustained or vocal opposition come from the American public. The wartime events produced an unjust result that visited great suffering upon an entire group of citizens, and upon resident aliens whom the Constitution also protects. While we do not analogize these events to the Holocaust—for the detention camps were not death camps—this is hardly cause for comfort in a democracy, even forty years later.

The belief that we Americans are exceptional often threatens our freedom by allowing us to look complacently at evil-doing elsewhere and to insist that "It can't happen here." Recalling the events of exclusion and detention, ensuring that later generations of Americans know this history, is critical immunization against infection by the virus of prejudice and the emotion of wartime struggle. "It did happen here" is a message that must be transmitted, not as an exercise in self-laceration but as an admonition for the future. Among our strengths as a nation is our willingness to acknowledge imperfection as well as to struggle for a more just society. It is in a spirit of continuing that struggle that the Commission recommends several forms of redress.

61

WILLIAM MINORU HOHRI

THE COMPLAINT

NCJAR's lawsuit was filed on March 16, 1983. For the first time in the history of the mass exclusion and detention of Japanese-Americans and their aftermath, the defendant is identified and the plaintiffs defined. For the first time in this history, we, the plaintiffs, spell out our injuries from our perspective, as the injured parties. There is no muting of our grievances as occurred with the WHEREAS statements written by Shosuke Sasaki for the 1979-80 Lowry Redress Bill. Our Complaint delineates allegation of fact upon allegation of fact in sharp, compelling language. We shed official euphemisms such as "evacuation" and "relocation centers" and replace them with "forced exclusion" and "prison camps." Our causes of action, the formal statement of charges, specify each constitutional and legal right that was violated. Nor are the remedies gratuitous as they were in the Evacuation Claims Act. We seek the maximum compensation allowed for our causes of action. We reject Congressman Jim Wright's proposed apology: "The best we can do, therefore, is to take official notice that what we did under the severe pressure of that wrenching emergency was completely out of character for us—to apologize to those on whom we inflicted the insulting assumption of their disloyalty and to avow that never again will any group of Americans be subjected to such humiliation on grounds no more valid than the blood that runs in their veins." Nor do we accept the words of Congressman George Danielson who merged the victims with victimizer: "The Government is the people." We move beyond the seemingly endless media and academic discussions on the nature and extent of the wrong and the many theories propounded which, while seeming to provide insight and enlightenment, often only promoted the propounder as the source of arcane knowledge. Instead of repressing our outrage for want of focus, we victims now have a lawsuit against the United States; we now have the proper means by which to channel our grievances and our demands for redress.

TWENTY-SEVEN BILLION

We are suing the United States of America for an unambiguously adversarial sum of twenty-seven billion dollars. The ante has been raised since 1979. The first Lowry Redress Bill had a projected cost of around three billion dollars. The ninefold increase of our action came not from a motive to sensationalize, but from the cumulative effect of the detailed allegations of facts and injuries embedded in our Complaint. These allegations coalesce into twenty-two causes of action. The magnitude of our prayer for relief, to use the legal expression, results from the multiplication of the class of 125,000 victims by twenty-two causes of action. We seek compensation of at least $10,000 for each cause of action. Twenty-two of them yield $220,000 per victim. Given the nature of the injuries, the individual claim is modest. This claim multiplied by 125,000 victims yields 27.5 billion dollars. Our Complaint is not addressing merely property losses. We are addressing injuries we sustained through the government's violation of our constitutional and civil rights. Client NCJAR had never given its law firm instruction on a bottom-line figure for monetary redress. The figure flows naturally from the compilation of historical facts which supported causes of actions. The figure is not a measure of lost property; it is a valuation of violated constitutional and civil rights. . . .

TWENTY-TWO CAUSES OF ACTION

Our lawsuit is impelled by twenty-two causes of action or counts. Like punch lines, they are the distillate of the dozens of allegations. Most are quite straightforward and easily understood. The first is entitled Due Process and states that what Japanese-Americans suffered they suffered "without individual hearings or the opportunity to be heard, in violation of the Fifth Amendment's guarantee that individuals shall not be deprived of life, liberty, or property without due process of law." The second, Equal Protection, is equally clear: Equal Protection was violated because the defendant acted "solely on the basis of race and national ancestry."

But the third, Unjust Taking, is more subtle. The Fifth Amendment states, "nor shall private property be taken for public use, without just compensation." This cause of action attempts to extend the idea of unjust taking from the destruction of our "real and personal property, commercial interests, livelihood, reputation, liberty, and other property rights," to "privileges, and entitlements secured by federal, state, and local law," charging that the defendant "failed to compensate or has provided grossly inadequate compensation for plaintiffs' losses of property rights." Our attorneys were anticipating the legal defense of sovereign immunity, whereby one may sue the government, the "sovereign," for monetary damages, only when the government consents to be sued. This Fifth Amendment clause mandates compensation. By this attempt to extend its meaning to encompass constitutional rights, our attorneys hoped to find a way around sovereign immunity.

The fourth count is based upon the Fourth Amendment's protection against unreasonable arrest, search, and seizure, an obvious violation. The fifth is based upon the privileges and immunities clause of Article 4, Section 2 of the Constitution:

The citizens of each state shall be entitled to all privileges and immunities of citizens in the several states . . .

This little-used clause is much like equal protection, and was plainly violated.

The sixth through the thirteenth counts are again quite direct. The sixth, based on the Sixth Amendment, is Right to Fair Trial and Representation by Counsel. It is difficult to believe that this failed to occur 125,000 times. The seventh states that the Eighth Amendment's protection from cruel and unusual punishment was violated, in that our treatment was "grossly disproportionate to any security risk . . . and, in light of the absence of the commission of any crime."

The eighth through eleventh counts are based upon the First Amendment. In the eighth count, we state that our First Amendment right to freedom of religion was violated with respect to the practice of Eastern religious beliefs. In the ninth, we state our denial of the Amendment's guarantee of freedom of speech and press. This refers to the prohibition of using the Japanese language in public meetings and censorship of camp newspapers. In the tenth, we state that we were not free to associate, again in violation of the First Amendment. In the eleventh, it is the Amendment's guarantee of Freedom of Petition for Redress of Grievances that is violated. When the WRA deemed inmates to be "troublemakers" and sent them to the Moab or Leupp isolation camps, these "troublemakers" were often no more than American citizens who demanded the redress of grievances. . . .

The fifteenth count is the final constitutional one: denial of *habeas corpus*, the right of a detained person to challenge the legality of his or her imprisonment. Not only was this right violated, but the government made a serious attempt to suspend *habeas corpus* through legislation in response to Mitsuye Endo's petition for freedom under *habeas corpus*. . . .

The Complaint was a solid achievement. It was a product of heart, mind, and soul. . . . But it had to undergo the twisting and tearing of adversarial challenge and judicial scrutiny. What would survive? Would anything?

62

JEANNE SAKATA

CORAM NOBIS
PRESS CONFERENCE

<u>TIME</u>
January 19, 1983

<u>CHARACTERS</u>

PETER IRONS, Caucasian, 41, Professor of Legal Studies

DALE MINAMI, Japanese American, 34, attorney

LORRAINE (LORI) BANNAI, Japanese American, 26, attorney

DON TAMAKI, Japanese American, 30s, attorney

FRED KOREMATSU, Japanese American, 62

SCENE NINETEEN

INT: SAN FRANCISCO PRESS CLUB. BACKSTAGE.

PETER: *(Narrating)* On the day we filed, Don had called a press conference to announce the reopening of Fred's historic case.

DON: *(Nervous)* Low expectations, OK guys? 'Cause I don't know if any of the press is even going to show up.

DALE: What the hell? You said you had the networks on the hook.

DON: Yeah I *did*. I played 'em against each other, told ABC and NBC that CBS was "following the story." Made 'em think it meant that CBS was actually *coming*, and it worked. "CBS will be there? OK we'll be there too." But in my follow up—man, I *lost* 'em. "This Japanese American prison thing, you're saying that happened HERE? You sure this isn't about, uh, Japanese prisoners of war?"

LORI: Everyone ready? *(Moving off—pushing back the curtain)* Okay here we go.

They enter the room. Journalists are everywhere.

INT: THE BUSY PRESS CLUB. JOURNALIST CROWD BUZZ

FX: CAMERAS CLICKING, FLASHES, MICROPHONE BEING TESTED.

DALE: You *guys*.

PETER: Holy cow, look at 'em.

DALE: *New York Times, Los Angeles Times, Baltimore Sun, San Francisco Examiner*—

DON: And all the networks. *(Fist pump) Yes.*

LORI: Dale. You're on. And Dale?

DALE: Yeah?

LORI: Don't screw this up.

DALE: *(Podium mic)* Welcome, everyone. Would everyone please have a seat.

FX: EVERYTHING QUIETS DOWN AS AUDIENCE TAKES THEIR SEATS

Today, we are filing these petitions for writ of error *coram nobis* to reopen cases which upheld the convictions of Minoru Yasui, Gordon Hirabayashi, and Fred Korematsu, and validated the forced removal and curfew orders which led to the imprisonment of 115,000 Japanese Americans during World War II.

The basis of our petitions is recently discovered evidence that indicates that high government officials suppressed, altered, and destroyed evidence in order to influence the outcomes of these cases at trial and on appeal, including appeals to the United States Supreme Court. Don?

DON: *(Podium mic)* We have here a unique opportunity to correct a wrong, where there was a gross violation of the civil liberties of Japanese Americans and an enormous toll of human suffering.

What we are asking here is not just for sympathy. We are asking for something very simple. That is, the justice that was denied these men 40 years ago.

And now, let's hear from Fred Korematsu.

FRED: *(Podium mic)* I was born here in Oakland, here, in the Bay Area, and I went to school here and learned all about the Constitution. I'm just like every other American; I wanted to stay here. And when this evacuation came, I felt that I was not a criminal or enemy alien, which I was classified as. And at the time of the evacuation, I stayed. I probably would assume that you, as American citizens, had they told you you had to get out, you'd feel the same way.

DALE: *(Podium mic)* Are there any questions?

REPORTERS #1, #2, AND #3: *(Off mic)* Here! I have a question! Question here!

Dale points to one of them.

DALE: Yes.

REPORTER 1: *(Off mic)* You are seeking to reopen cases decided by the Supreme Court in the 1940s?

DALE: We are.

REPORTER 2: *(Off mic)* And you are doing that through an obscure legal process called—what?

DALE: *Coram nobis.* A very rarely used proceeding that can be used to attack a criminal conviction.

REPORTERS: *(Sounds of disbelief)*

REPORTER 3: *(Off mic)* Are you all serious?

DALE: Dead serious.

A monetary sum and words alone cannot restore lost years or erase painful memories; neither can they fully convey our Nation's resolve to rectify injustice and to uphold the rights of individuals. We can never fully right the wrongs of the past. But we can take a clear stand for justice and recognize that serious injustices were done to Japanese Americans during World War II.

In enacting a law calling for restitution and offering a sincere apology, your fellow Americans have, in a very real sense, renewed their traditional commitment to the ideals of freedom, equality, and justice. You and your family have our best wishes for the future.

Sincerely,

/s/ George Bush

traci kato-kiriyama

NO REDRESS

(dedicated to ALL the ancestors who died before
knowing that Redress & Reparations would be a
thing to come or to be fought for in the future we
call now)

no museum

no monument

no poem
no song
can house
the spirit
of a passed soul
like that of my
grandfather
who died before
justice
could meet
the old man
at his mailbox

Grandpa
never got to
stand in line
at the bank
three inches

taller
with Redress check
in hand
one foot in front
of the other feeling
grounded again

never got to deposit
an apology
in
his savings account

never got to wonder
of how he might
spend
this money
on new equipment
for the nursery or
a truck for himself or
college money for
his grandchildren
or
for once
take
the most
takai cuts
from the fish truck man

most years
in April

I attend
Pilgrimage

I say
Hello, Manzanar

I bow at the graves

I speak to the wind
of my hopes
for
Afterlife
to be a real thing

not so I can see
Grandpa again

but for him
to look around today, jump
into the circle, dance
the Tanko Bushi
and watch
me get it right

and see our friends
all our relations
learn what we mean by
chosen family
we are here

not only to remember

but to remind the local docents
this place will never
be a museum

this body will never
forget

and we leave Pilgrimage
with pledges as concrete
as the monument

we sing songs
to keep each other awake
on the long ride home

we lose sight quickly
rearview mirrors
a pitch black sky

where they close the gate
at the hour
they have had enough of us

where we leave behind
parts of our
best poetry

where I hope not
but
think
grandpa
sits
still
waiting

Repeating History

64

PERRY MIYAKE

EVACUATION, THE SEQUEL

BUDDHAHEAD STANDARD TIME

David took side streets out of Gardena—once the largest Japanese American community in the U.S., a ghost town now—still enough daylight so he wouldn't be driving too close to the airport, a federal offense for Japanese since ReVac.

He was in no hurry because he knew his brother John was on Buddhahead standard time. Late. Late for his wedding, for his divorce proceedings, for the birth of his daughter.

He drove past the billboards, stills from the commercials running on TV, only without the music swelling patriotically in the background.

"We're starting all over again, America."

"Look out, America's back and it's not Japanese."

And your basic, "Buy American, Screw Japan."

Beautiful photography, bold message in bold lettering, faces of all colors marching together, dissolving into one another. Very "United We Stand," slightly tweaked.

Americans of all colors. White, black, brown, occasionally red, and yellow if they didn't look Japanese.

Reaching a pinnacle, working together, making a difference, all people of almost all races, bringing tears to your eyes as you vow to . . . buy something with an American name on it, or borrow money from a bank with a real American name. So what if it's owned by the British or Dutch or Italians? Their accents are better than those gummy, toothy Japanese.

ReVac was no surprise. Executive Order 9066 revisited.

World War III became the Economic War with Japan. If the economy went down the toilet, the terrorists would have won.

If World War II was the battle to save Western Civilization from the Nazi party and the Japanese race, World War III—the Economic War became the ultimate battle to save the very soul of America: its pocketbook.

Unlike September 11, this enemy was immediately identifiable; the same economic foe, the same arch-enemy of the United States since December 7, 1941—Japan.

Restrictions became sanctions and eventually became a total ban of all Japanese products, which only made things worse.

Unemployment rose above thirty percent.

The President needed a dramatic revelation to push the concept of World War III—the Economic War into the hyperspace of public support.

Like FDR, he needed his Pearl Harbor.

It came in the form of a two-pronged rumor:

One, that the AIDS virus had originally been developed by Japanese scientists during World War II atrocity experiments conducted on captured civilians and Allied POWs. This accusation, although contrary to the conspiracy theories linking AIDS as a man-made tool of the Reagan-Bush right-wing anti-sex era, became a staple of the Internet, TV tabloid shows, radio talk shows and the other popular vehicles responsible for the mass dissemination of information. It divided liberals better than the O.J. trial.

And two, that the source of modern bioterrorist weapons being used against the American people could be traced to these same World War II Japanese atrocity experiments.

The war was on.

All Japanese businesses were expelled, investments confiscated. Japanese citizens who hadn't already left were deported.

Unemployment went up past forty percent.

It was a well-greased ugly slide as slanty-eyed, bucktoothed accent jokes started showing up regularly on network TV shows, unprotested, then familiar and accepted as humor. From there it was a natural regression from ridicule to dehumanization to blame, a small step from "Buy American" to "Blame the Japanese" to "Kill the Japs." As the economy sank like a stone, America got ugged out by anything Japanese and finally scrapped the last vestige of constitutional sanctuary against anything vaguely Japanese, and if anything was vaguely Japanese, it was a Japanese American.

Given the historical inability of mainstream America to distinguish an American of Japanese ancestry from a foreign Japanese national, David knew they were next.

The President signed Executive Order 9066-A, instructing persons of Japanese ancestry to sacrifice their jobs to real Americans by leaving the country, or be subject to Re-Evacuation, New and Improved.

The JACL filed suit in court to get a pre-emptive stay against ReVac but all their civil liberties lawyers, ex-judges, ex-Senators, ex-Representatives, ex-mayors, and ex-Cabinet members couldn't stop a presidential order in time of war. The wheels were already turning.

David was glad all his aunts and uncles and his Mom and Dad and any Nisei born and raised in America and gone through it once weren't here the second time around. Uncle Mas caught some shrapnel in France and limped for the rest of his life until the shrapnel ate away his intestines and, fifty years later, killed him. Purple Heart, Silver Star, went to all the 442nd reunions and VFW functions. David was glad Uncle Mas didn't see the official notice, this time billboard high and glo-lit, that David and his generation had only seen in uncensored history books:

INSTRUCTIONS
TO ALL PERSONS OF
JAPANESE
ANCESTRY

65

FRED KOREMATSU

DO WE REALLY NEED TO RELEARN THE LESSONS OF JAPANESE AMERICAN INTERNMENT?

In 1942, I was arrested and convicted for being a Japanese American trying to live here in the Bay Area. The day after my arrest a newspaper headline declared, "Jap Spy Arrested in San Leandro."

Of course, I was no spy. The government never charged me with being a spy. I was a U.S. citizen born and raised in Oakland. I even tried to enlist in the Coast Guard (they didn't take me because of my race). But my citizenship and my loyalty did not matter to the federal government. On Feb. 19, 1942, anyone of Japanese heritage was ordered excluded from the West Coast. I was charged and convicted of being a Japanese American living in an area in which all people of my ancestry had been ordered to be interned.

I fought my conviction at that time. My case went to the U.S. Supreme Court, but in 1944 my efforts to seek protection under the Constitution were rejected.

After I was released in 1945, my criminal record continued to affect my life. It was hard to find work. I was considered to be a criminal. It took almost 40 years and the efforts of many people to reopen my case. In 1983, a federal court judge found that the government had hidden evidence and lied to the Supreme Court during my appeal. The judge found that Japanese Americans were not the threat that the government publicly claimed. My criminal record was removed.

As my case was being reconsidered by the courts, again as a result of the efforts of many people across the country, Congress created a commission to study the exclusion and incarceration of Japanese Americans. The commission found that no Japanese American had been involved in espionage or sabotage and that no military necessity existed to imprison us. Based on the commission's findings and of military historians who reconsidered the original records from the war, Congress passed the Civil Liberties Act of 1988, declaring that the internment of Japanese Americans was unjustified. Finally, it seemed that the burden of being accused of being an "enemy race" had been lifted from our shoulders.

But now the old accusations are back. Fox News media personality Michelle Malkin claims that some Japanese Americans were spies during World War II. Based upon her suspicions, Malkin claims the internment of all Japanese Americans was not such a bad idea after all. She goes on to claim that racial profiling of Arab Americans today is justified by the need to fight terrorism. According to Malkin, it is OK to take away an entire ethnic group's civil rights because some individuals are suspect. Malkin argues for reviving the old notion of guilt by association.

It is painful to see reopened for serious debate the question of whether the government was justified in imprisoning Japanese Americans during World War II. It was my hope that my case and the cases of other Japanese American internees would be remembered for the dangers of racial and ethnic scapegoating.

Fears and prejudices directed against minority communities are too easy to evoke and exaggerate, often to serve the political agendas of those who promote those fears. I know what it is like to be at the other end of such scapegoating and how difficult it is to clear one's name after unjustified suspicions are endorsed as fact by the government. If someone is a spy or terrorist they should be prosecuted for their actions. But no one should ever be locked away simply because they share the same race, ethnicity, or religion as a spy or terrorist. If that principle was not learned from the internment of Japanese Americans, then these are very dangerous times for our democracy.

66

BRANDON SHIMODA

WE HAVE BEEN HERE
BEFORE

On Saturday, June 22, 2019, a group of Japanese Americans gathered in front of Bentley Gate, on the edge of Fort Sill, an army base outside Lawton, Oklahoma, to protest the Trump administration's plan to use the base to incarcerate approximately 1,600 asylum-seeking migrant children from Central America. Among the Japanese Americans were several elders in their 70s and 80s, for whom the site possessed a harrowing correspondence to their own childhoods.

The first to speak was Satsuki Ina, a writer, filmmaker, therapist, and activist. "I am a former child incarceree," she began. Seventy-seven years ago, "120,000 of us were removed from our homes and forcefully incarcerated in prison camps across the country." Ina was born in one of the prison camps: Tule Lake, in California, which was one of the 10 main concentration camps, and served as a maximum-security prison for Japanese Americans classified as disloyal. Ina was born into the impossible status of being simultaneously a citizen and an enemy of the United States.

"We were in American concentration camps," she continued. "We were held under indefinite detention. We were without due process of law. We were charged without any evidence of being a threat to national security, that we were an unassimilable race, that we would be a threat to the economy. We hear these exact words today regarding innocent people seeking asylum in this country."

Her testimony was followed by that of other elders, each wearing a #StopRepeatingHistory T-shirt, and each stating the name of the camp in which they had been incarcerated. They were all, at the time, children, some of them infants. And though 77 years had passed, along with many cycles of traumatization and healing, the imminent resurrection of Fort Sill as a concentration camp for children exposed those years, and the history they held back, as a single, unrelieved wound.

Ina and the Japanese Americans were speaking not only on behalf of themselves, but on behalf of the 707 Japanese immigrants who were incarcerated at Fort Sill between 1941 and 1942. ("Interned" is the legal term for the imprisonment of noncitizens, but I prefer "incarcerated," because Asian immigrants were ineligible, by law, to attain citizenship; "incarcerated," therefore, emphasizes the impossibility of their situation.) That was far from the beginning of Fort Sill's carceral history. It was established in 1869 to control the Indigenous populations on the surrounding land. For 20 years, between 1894 and 1914, approximately 340 Chiricahua Apaches were incarcerated as prisoners of war at Fort Sill. Among them was the Apache leader Geronimo, who is buried there. Fort Sill was also the site of a Native American compulsory boarding school, which separated Indigenous children from their families and communities, forcing them into a program of cultural erasure and reidentification. Opened in 1871, the school was not closed until 1980. Fort Sill also incarcerated migrant children during the Obama administration.

I enter history through its graveyard. I first heard of Fort Sill because of a man named Ichiro Shimoda. Shimoda—Issei, or first-generation Japanese immigrant—was a 45-year-old gardener from Los Angeles who died in Fort Sill. His story, which exists in the historical record in contradictory fragments, is that he witnessed the murder of another Issei, Kanesaburo Oshima, a shopkeeper from Hawaii, who was shot and killed by the guards. According to one account, Shimoda suffered a nervous breakdown as a result, and was taken to the military hospital, where he died. None of the other prisoners were with him, and nothing else about the incident is known. Shimoda's death, with Oshima's murder, was folded efficiently into the oblivion on which the concentration camp system thrived. No guards stood trial or were otherwise held accountable.

I first heard of Shimoda because, prior to Fort Sill, he had been incarcerated in a Department of Justice prison in Missoula, Montana, with another Shimoda: my grandfather, Midori Shimoda. When I was young, I did not know my grandfather had once been classified as an enemy alien (#1128762) of the country I took for granted as my own. My grandfather was incarcerated in Fort Missoula under suspicion of being a spy for Japan. He was a photographer, and a Japanese immigrant, which made him congenitally guilty in the mind of the US government. Other members of my family had also been incarcerated: my great-aunt Joy in Poston, Arizona; my great-uncle Makeo, great-aunt Tsuruyo, and their daughters, Carole and Sally, in Heart Mountain, Wyoming. As a child, I was not aware of these foundational facts, nor about the incarceration of Japanese Americans in general. My family was silent on the subject. I was too young to understand their silence as the form of speaking they had chosen, or felt forced to choose— which cultivated in me a belief that the future not only meant more than the past but even required the obliteration of the past to be realized.

The Civil Liberties Act of 1988, the culmination of a multi-generational fight to attain recognition and redress for those who had been incarcerated, allowed for reparations. Eighty-two thousand two hundred and nineteen Japanese American citizens and legal residents each received $20,000 from the United States government as recompense for what they had lost. Or, because "loss" is, in this case, a euphemism for "theft," they received restitution for a fraction of what had been stolen. My grandmother (Nisei, or second generation, who lived, during the war, in Utah, and therefore avoided incarceration) used my grandfather's reparations to pay for one year's rent at the nursing home where he spent the last years of his life. The check came with a boilerplate apology from President George H. W. Bush: "You and your family have our best wishes for the future," it said. Five years later, my grandfather was dead.

The silence in which he passed suggested, to me, that the price of citizenship was forgetting, and that forgetting was annihilative. Yet his death released in me a torrent of questions about his struggle to become a citizen, and exposed the gravity of my citizenship as both the legacy and the purgatorial afterlife of his experience as an enemy alien. My grandfather struggled his entire life to establish for himself and his family a place in the American scenario, and achieved some version of that place, but at the expense of permitting himself an understanding of the American scenario as a myth predicated on the extinguishing of souls.

Today's migrant concentration camps are incontestable proof of the myth, and of the extinguishing. The migrant children—many of whom crossed the US-Mexico border with family members, half of them with parents already in the United States, and yet who are classified as unaccompanied minors—are proof. What happens to migrant children in a place like Fort Sill? What happened there to the generations of Indigenous children, to the Chiricahua Apaches, to the Japanese immigrants? What is happening in the concentration camps and prisons and jails and incarceration and detention sites that extend across the country?

Concentration camps are basic units of space the United States has devised for the populations it sees as unassimilable, incongruous with—and threatening to—its self-image. Concentration camps can be, and have been, invented, at will, from sites—military bases to empty box stores—retained for use in the event of a crisis, sometimes real, though more often manufactured. They are outposts of the border wall, therefore materializations of the white settler hatred and rage by which the border wall, and its innumerable chimeras, are motivated. And we are, right now, watching the United States resurrect, with frightening ease, its system of concentration camps, and all the crimes against humanity such a system entails. With this resurrection, the government is coordinating, in the digestible guise of bureaucratic chaos, the disintegration of communities, families, individuals, languages, cultures, physical and mental health, futures. Reliant upon the prevention-through-deterrence method of control, this approach to migration should be considered a form of ethnic cleansing by attrition.

Children are being taken from their families by the US government. They are being held in cages. They are being moved from these overcrowded cages to more indefinite, less visible—and apparently, for some, more acceptable—concentration camps. And they are being deprived of the basic dignities—clean water, warmth, safety, sleep, stimulation, health care, the assurance of being reunited with their parents, their families—that might, in their isolation, remind them that there is, beyond the care they are able to offer each other, a world, and that the world cares.

The Japanese American elders are among the centuries of oppressed peoples of this country who have absorbed and remember this truth. I wrote to Satsuki Ina to ask her how she felt being at Fort Sill. "I found my suffocated voice," she wrote back. Though she was not incarcerated there, it was as though her childhood, having been arrested at Tule Lake, had been fractured and dispersed across the nation's geography of incarceration, and that her voice, preceding her, was waiting. "Anger rose to the top of the sorrow."

A month after the Japanese American elders gathered on the edge of Fort Sill, they returned. On July 20, a coalition of more than 400 protesters, including Buddhist priests, immigrant youth, and members of Indigenous, Latinx, Black, Jewish, and Asian American activist communities, gathered to protest. Four days later, on July 24, Oklahoma Senator Jim Inhofe announced that the plan to use the base to incarcerate migrant children was being put on hold. Two days after that, the Administration for Children and Families, a division of the Department of Health and Human Services, confirmed that, due to a decrease in migrant children crossing the border, there was no longer "an immediate need to place children in influx facilities." It is important to define these reversals, for the protesters in particular, as victories, which they are. But it is also important to consider that as much as they are victories, they are also occasions for the machinery of incarceration, under cover of false appeasement and bureaucracy, to retaliate, shapeshift, and keep running.

"Injustice anywhere is a threat to justice everywhere," wrote Martin Luther King Jr., on scraps of paper and a newspaper smuggled to him in a jail in Birmingham, Alabama, 1963. The intercoalitional protests at Fort Sill—along with Japanese American–led protests in the ruins of the Department of Justice prison in Crystal City, Texas; at the detention center in Dilley, Texas; in Japantown in Los Angeles, San Francisco, San Jose, everywhere—are the expression of traumas and their echoes that are as much a source of solidarity as they are the coordinated product of American violence. The elements that made possible, and inevitable, the incarceration of 120,000 Japanese immigrants and Japanese American citizens during WWII, are, as Satsuki Ina reminded us, still operational. They are still being deployed, in both flagrant and subliminal ways, across the spectrum of American existence.

As I think about my grandfather, and the ways he was forced into silence; as I think about the ways my grandfather's silence haunts my understanding of what it means to be a citizen; as I think about the elders, and the ways their voices have, by the present conditions of their trauma and witness, been newly compelled; as I think about the descendants, like myself, who are uncovering, within the capacity of our inheritance, those facets of injustice which are, in this country, despairingly constitutional; and as I think about the migrants, the people, who are attempting, with tremendous hope, to fashion a future out of their desperation, I am led to believe that Japanese American incarceration, as one example, one blueprint, in an unremitting and interminable system, has not ended. It has entered a new phase.

67

BRYNN SAITO

THESES ON THE PHILOSOPHY OF HISTORY

or *Listening to the Presidential Debate While Stuck in Traffic*

1.

Roads clog with people in vehicles crossing the Golden Gate
Give my rage back to me, I know how to hold it
Ghost fog grows and stretches itself through the bars and I'm
  ready for it
On my radio, the white general and the white general
yank each other into the deep end, good heavens
Don't teach me to hate my language tonight
Don't teach me how to hate my lips and their language
  tonight
Tongo says capitalism walks on water, I've seen my TV,
  I believe it
All of the redwoods in the world can't keep this country from
  wanting to die
The future has arrived and it's doubled over
and the best of us are ready for love though we're burning

2.

Roads clog with people in vehicles crossing the Golden Gate
My family is Eduardo and Mitsuo and Marilyn and Alma

and Samuel and Fumio and the twin who drank himself to
   death
and the auntie who drank herself to death
and the Issei and the Nisei and the Sansei with their rock
   faces and nightmares
Undisguise me, said the stone
Undisguise me, said the stone to the desert light
Undisguise me, said the stone to the river
Lay me down under harsh water flowing under midnight
   starlight
Take my face off of my face, said the stone, shake me open

3.

Roads clog with people in vehicles crossing the Golden Gate
The white general and the white general
teach me how to hate my language on the radio tonight
Which nightmare of a framework makes the human count
Which bodies count and which count against
Grandma met Grandpa in those camps
Let me give your rage back to you, said the poem
Stop trying so damn hard, said the poem
Everything that has ever happened to you and your family
keeps happening and the love keeps coming in with its
   surgery
Get good with yourself, said the poem, get gone

68

FRANK ABE, TAMIKO NIMURA,
ROSS ISHIKAWA, MATT SASAKI

NEVER AGAIN IS NOW

At UCLA after the war, I wore a pork pie hat to appear eccentric and keep others from putting me on the spot with the inevitable, awkward question ...

So, which camp were you in?

Yes, I was in Tule Lake.

I'm not proud of it, but I'm not ashamed ... are you trying to make me feel ashamed?

As a citizen of no nation, it was hard to get a job but I was finally hired as a librarian.

Wayne Collins kept filing affidavits until the Justice Department finally restored my citizenship in 1959. All those years, I felt it was my fault.

But after 35 years, can you imagine my chagrin, my dismay, when I learned there was no law that required draft-age Nisei to answer that loyalty questionnaire in camp? All those threats of prison and fines ... all lies. I was angry all over again.

YEARS OF INFAMY

At least I'm thankful for the opportunity to unburden myself with others who were cast out from our own community, even to this day.

To be an American is a privilege I appreciate ... and if there's one thing I've learned, it's that America must unburden itself too.

The government was wrong to single us out for exclusion based solely on our race. It was wrong then, and it would be wrong now.

And whenever we see America turn against a people because of their race, or their religion, or their whatever, we won't just stand by. We won't just go along.

IT HAPPENED TO US.
WE REFUSE TO LET IT HAPPEN AGAIN.

Acknowledgments

We could not have created an anthology of this size and scope without the generosity of the contributors who shared their work and the families and publishers of deceased authors who provided biographical information and permissions for use. Thank you.

Junko Kobayashi first introduced us to *Tessaku*, the literary magazine of the Tule Lake Segregation Center, through her doctoral thesis, "'Bitter Sweet Home': Celebration of Biculturalism in Japanese Language Japanese American Literature, 1936–1952." The translations we commissioned for this volume by Andrew Way Leong are based upon reproductions of camp literary magazines published in 1997 by Fuji Shuppan of Tokyo in the thirteen-volume set *Nikkei Amerika bungaku zasshi shūsei*, edited by Satae Shinoda and Iwao Yamamoto. We drew information from Shinoda's preface thanks to a new translation by Lisa Hofmann-Kuroda for the *Tessaku* Community Advisory Board and Translation Collective.

Brian Niiya and Greg Robinson provided detailed notes on the manuscript. For critical suggestions and contributions, we thank Konrad Aderer, Erin Aoyama, Takako Day, Tara Fickle, Art Hansen, Heather Hathaway, Kimberly Kono, Minoru Kanda, Alan Ota, Bill E. Peterson, Vince Schleitwiler, Jolie Sheffer, Hiroshi Shimizu, John Streamas, Stephen Sumida, Linda Tamura, Jonathan van Harmelen, Patricia Wakida, Yuriko Yamaki, Stan Yogi, and readers and friends in such groups as Densho, the Association for Asian American Studies, the Five College Asian/Pacific/American Studies Program, and the many organized camp pilgrimages.

Financial and structural support from Smith College was essential to the production of this volume. Student research assistants worked with us throughout the process of recovery, sifting, and editing, and for that we are grateful to Kristina Chang, Claire Cheung, Miche Hu, Emma Kemp, Natalia Perkins, Lydia Sheyda, Christine Qian, Sarah Yamashita, and Katarina Yuan. Smith College librarians assisted us with accessing and acquiring primary texts; special thanks go to Martin Antonetti, Matthew Durand, Elizabeth Myers, Christina Ryan, Pamela Skinner, Shannon Supple, Dominique Tremblay, and Lucinda Williams.

For championing this volume and bringing it to print, we are deeply indebted to the keen insight and unwavering encouragement of our editor, Elda Rotor, vice president and publisher of Penguin Classics.

Finally, Frank wishes to thank Laureen Mar, and Floyd wishes to thank Sheri Cheung, for their patience and support throughout the compiling of this work.

Suggestions for
Further Exploration

For a basic understanding and overview of the wartime incarceration, Densho.org provides video oral histories with firsthand accounts of all aspects of the camp experience, accompanied by archival photos and primary documents. Peer-reviewed materials explore all aspects of the history, including the ABCs of the incarceration, a searchable encyclopedia, a guide to terminology, and a resource guide for educators with books and films sortable by theme and grade level. Our suggestions below will help you go even deeper into the themes covered by Densho and presented in this volume.

PART I: BEFORE CAMP

Arrival and Community

To appreciate the racism and hostile legislation encountered by the early migrants, see *The Issei: The World of the First Generation Japanese Immigrants (1885–1924)* by Yuji Ichioka (1988), *Strangers from a Different Shore: A History of Asian Americans* by Ronald Takaki (1990), and *Yellow Peril!: An Archive of Anti-Asian Fear*, edited by John Kuo Wei Tchen and Dylan Yeats (2014).

Arrest and Alien Internment

The FBI's targeting of Buddhism as incompatible with American values is laid bare in *American Sutra: A Story of Faith and Freedom in the Second World War* by Duncan Ryūken

Williams (2019). Williams also developed the Irei project to identify and record the names of the more than 125,000 incarcerated persons in a sacred Ireichō book and a searchable database at ireizo.com. Recent translations have made accessible memoirs in Japanese by Issei who were sent to Army and Department of Justice alien internment camps, including *Life Behind Barbed Wire: The World War II Internment Memoirs of a Hawai'i Issei* by Yasutaro Soga (2008), *An Internment Odyssey: Haisho Tenten* by Suikei Furuya (2017), *Family Torn Apart: The Internment Story of the Otokichi Muin Ozaki Family*, edited by Gail Honda (2012), and *Taken from the Paradise Isle: The Hoshida Family Story*, edited by Heidi Kim (2015).

Cooperation and Refusal

Greg Robinson's *By Order of the President: FDR and the Internment of Japanese Americans* (2001) shows how Roosevelt's racial view of the Japanese in America as immutably foreign and threatening informed his decisions for mass exclusion and incarceration. The National JACL in 1990 conducted its own investigation into its wartime policy of cooperation with the government; the unexpurgated version of what's come to be known as "The Lim Report" can be found at resisters.com /JACL, along with the full text of memos in this volume from Mike Masaoka. The refusal of Fred Korematsu, Gordon Hirabayashi, and Min Yasui to comply with expulsion is documented in Steven Okazaki's Academy Award–nominated film, *Unfinished Business* (1985).

PART II: THE CAMPS

Foundational studies that have stood the test of time include Michi Nishiura Weglyn's *Years of Infamy: The Untold Story of America's Concentration Camps* (1976), the first comprehensive history of the incarceration written by a Nisei working with government documents from the National Archives, and *Concentration Camps USA: Japanese Americans and World*

War II by Roger Daniels (1971), the book that first held to account the government officials responsible for the exclusion and incarceration. Lawson Fusao Inada and Patricia Wakida curate a wealth of additional readings in their anthology, *Only What We Could Carry: The Japanese American Internment Experience* (2014).

Fairgrounds and Racetracks

Miné Okubo's much-reprinted drawings in *Citizen 13660* (1946) convey the emotional impact of arriving at the Tanforan Racetrack, and her later journey to Topaz. The army's hasty construction of the WCCA assembly centers is detailed in the study of one such site, *Camp Harmony: Seattle's Japanese Americans and the Puyallup Assembly Center* by Louis Fiset (2009).

Deserts and Swamps

The construction of civilian War Relocation Centers on Indigenous lands is examined in *Sharing a Desert Home: Life on the Colorado River Indian Reservation, Poston, Arizona, 1942–1945* by Ruth Y. Okimoto (2001) and Iyko Day's "Settler Colonialism in Asian North American Representation" in *The Oxford Encyclopedia of Asian American Literature and Culture* (2020). Daily life in the camps is well described by Yoshiko Uchida in *Desert Exile: The Uprooting of a Japanese American Family* (1982), Toyo Suyemoto in *I Call to Remembrance: Toyo Suyemoto's Years of Internment* (2007), and in *The Evacuation Diary of Hatsuye Egami* (1995). The tension between photographs taken of incarcerees and the reality of their experience is uncovered in Jasmine Alinder's *Moving Images: Photography and the Japanese American Incarceration* (2011) and Elena Tajima Creef's *Imaging Japanese America: The Visual Construction of Citizenship, Nation, and the Body* (2004). Heather Hathaway's *That Damned Fence: The Literature of the Japanese American Prison Camps* (2022) is an essential study of the literary magazines at five camps: *TREK* and *All Aboard* from Topaz, *Pulse* from Amache, *The Pen* from

Rohwer, Jerome's *Magnet*, and *The Tulean Dispatch*. The Heart Mountain Wyoming Foundation has translated issues of the *Heart Mountain Bungei* literary magazine and shared them at exhibits.heartmountain.org/bungei. Disturbances in the camps are brought to light in *Barbed Voices: Oral History, Resistance, and the World War II Japanese American Social Disaster* by Arthur A. Hansen (2018). A popular retelling of the Manzanar revolt appears in the classroom favorite *Farewell to Manzanar* by Jeanne Wakatsuki Houston and James D. Houston (1973) and in the 1976 NBC/Universal film based on the book, available on DVD only from the Japanese American National Museum store in Los Angeles. The Wakasa shooting at Topaz was imagined visually by artists Miné Okubo and Chiura Obata; researchers in 2020 discovered the site where mourners had buried a large memorial stone and they share that story at wakasamemorial.org. The exclusion order forbade the bringing of pets, but beloved animals were later shipped by friends, and those found at the camps could be adopted; see bit.ly/3HOM0VD.

Registration and Segregation

Eric L. Muller's *American Inquisition: The Hunt for Japanese American Disloyalty in World War II* (2007) reveals the origins of the loyalty questionnaire and the mechanics of loyalty screening the government deployed against its own citizens. A concise overview of Tule Lake and its conversion to a WRA segregation center can be found in Barbara Takei and Judy Tachibana's *Tule Lake Revisited: A Brief History and Guide to the Tule Lake Concentration Camp Site* (2012). *The Spoilage: Japanese American Evacuation and Resettlement* by Dorothy S. Thomas and Richard Nishimoto (1946) preserves valuable statements from segregees and stockade inmates, while Takako Day conducted interviews in Japanese with the Kibei at Tule Lake for *Show Me the Way to Go Home: The Moral Dilemma of Kibei No No Boys in World War Two Incarceration Camps* (2014). Satiric firsthand observations fill the short stories of WRA social worker Barney Shallit collected in *Song of Anger: Tales of Tule Lake* (2001).

Volunteers and the Draft

The valor of the Nisei soldiers is saluted in countless books, such as *Nisei Soldiers Break Their Silence: Coming Home to Hood River* by Linda Tamura (2012) and *Facing the Mountain* by Daniel James Brown (2022), and such films as *Armed with Language* (2021), written and co-produced by David Mura about the Military Intelligence Service Language School. The story behind the Mothers Society of Minidoka is recovered by Mira Shimabukuro in *Relocating Authority: Japanese Americans Writing to Redress Mass Incarceration* (2015). John Okada's landmark novel, *No-No Boy* (1957), conveys the struggle of a draft resister trying to find his place upon returning home from prison after the war; Okada based his protagonist on draft resister Jim Akutsu, the son of Nao Akutsu, as established in *John Okada: The Life & Rediscovered Work of the Author of No-No Boy* (2018), edited by Abe, Robinson, and Cheung. Akutsu's "kangaroo court" trial in Idaho is recounted in Eric L. Muller's *Free to Die for Their Country: The Story of the Japanese American Draft Resisters in World War II* (2001). The only organized draft resistance, that of the Heart Mountain Fair Play Committee, is covered in depth in Frank Chin's *Born in the USA: A Story of Japanese America, 1889–1947* (2002), James Omura's *Nisei Naysayer: The Memoir of Militant Japanese American Journalist Jimmie Omura*, edited by Art Hansen (2018), and Abe's film, *Conscience and the Constitution* (2000).

Resegregation and Renunciation

Second Kinenhi: Reflections on Tule Lake by the Tule Lake Committee (2000) contains essential interviews and photographs documenting the marching and bugling of the *Hokoku Hoshi-dan* and the violent arrests of segregee leaders. The origins and outcome of the renunciation crisis are laid out in the memoir of Minoru Kiyota, *Beyond Loyalty: The Story of a Kibei* (1997) and in graphic novel form in the Tule Lake sections of *We Hereby Refuse: Japanese American Resistance to Wartime Incarceration* (2021).

PART III: AFTER CAMP

Resettlement and Reconnection

The adjustments incarcerees had to make coming out of the camps are deeply felt in "Wilshire Bus" by Hisaye Yamamoto in *Seventeen Syllables and Other Stories* (1998) and in "The Sensei" by Wakako Yamauchi in *Songs My Mother Taught Me: Stories, Plays, and Memoir* (1994). Broader examinations of resettlement are in Greg Robinson's *After Camp: Portraits in Midcentury Japanese American Life and Politics* (2012) and *Life After Manzanar* by Naomi Hirahara and Heather C. Lindquist (2018). Hirahara has also written two historical mystery novels that humanize the experience of resettlement in Chicago in *Clark and Division* (2021) and the return of families to Los Angeles in *Evergreen* (2023). As a Sansei, novelist Julie Otsuka blends research with family memory to imagine the inner lives of Issei picture brides from arrival up to their expulsion in *The Buddha in the Attic* (2011), of incarcerees from expulsion to imprisonment in *When the Emperor Was Divine* (2002), and of the fading memory of camp in *The Swimmers* (2022). Camp pilgrimages provide a means for descendants to personally sense the isolation and unforgiving landscapes at the sites of incarceration; the team at Japanese American Memorial Pilgrimages provides a clearinghouse for information on upcoming events at jampilgrimages.com. Personal and family trauma can be passed down through generations, as seen in the documentaries, *Children of the Camps* by Satsuki Ina (1999) and *History and Memory: For Akiko and Takashige* by Rea Tajiri (1991), and in Donna Nagata's study of the Sansei, *Legacy of Injustice: Exploring the Cross-Generational Impact of the Japanese American Internment* (1993); highlights of Nagata's research on the Yonsei appear in *Show Me the Way to Go to Home* by Sandy Sugawara and Catiana Garcia Kilroy (2023), an art book with haunting photographs of the present-day ruins of all ten WRA camps.

Redress

The campaign for justice was pursued on many fronts, from *Born in Seattle* by Robert Shimabukuro (2001) to the organizing in Los Angeles detailed in *NCRR: The Grassroots Struggle for Japanese American Redress and Reparations* by Nikkei for Civil Rights & Redress (2018). The JACL lobbied at the national level, as former national director John Tateishi recounts in *Redress: The Inside Story of the Successful Campaign for Japanese American Redress* (2020). Historians Aiko Herzig-Yoshinaga and Peter Irons independently discovered documents in the National Archives showing how the War Department suppressed evidence of Japanese American innocence in World War II. Irons laid out the strategy to reopen the Supreme Court convictions of Fred Korematsu, Gordon Hirabayashi, and Min Yasui in *Justice at War: The Story of the Japanese American Internment Cases* (1983), and compiled the key court briefs in *Justice Delayed: The Record of the Japanese American Internment Cases* (1989).

Repeating History

The economic anxiety that fed anti-Asian resentment in the 1980s is captured in the Academy Award–nominated film *Who Killed Vincent Chin?* by Renee Tajima-Peña and Christine Choy (1987). Links between the incarceration and racial and religious abuses in the so-called war on terror post-9/11 are drawn in *Race, Rights, and National Security: Law and the Japanese American Incarceration* (2021) by Eric Yamamoto, Lorraine Bannai, and Margaret Chon. More recently, Satsuki Ina went undercover at family detention centers near the southern border to report on the severity of the trauma on women and children there in "I Know an American 'Internment' Camp When I See One" at bit.ly/44FP7ZZ. Ina is also co-founder of "Tsuru for Solidarity," tsuruforsolidarity.org, which unites Japanese American allies who stand on the moral authority of the incarceration experience to take direct action in support of immigrant and refugee communities to end detention sites.

About the Authors

Frank Abe (b. 1951; script and story; father in Heart Mountain), **Tamiko Nimura** (b. 1973; story; father and uncle in Tule Lake), **Ross Ishikawa** (b. 1962; artwork; father in Amache), and **Matt Sasaki** (b. 1961; artwork; parents in Minidoka) created the graphic novel *We Hereby Refuse: Japanese American Resistance to Wartime Incarceration* (2021) for the Wing Luke Museum of Seattle.

Yoshio Abe (1911–1980) was born in Portland, Oregon, and imprisoned at Santa Anita and Amache. A Kibei Nisei educated in Japan, he returned there in 1960 and wrote *The Man of Dual Nationality (Nijyu kokuseki sha)*, a novel in three volumes (1971).

Motomu Akashi (1929–2012) was born in Merced, California, and imprisoned at Tanforan, Topaz, and Tule Lake. As the son of a resegregationist leader, he expatriated with his family to Japan in 1946, but returned in 1948 and enlisted in the U.S. Army. He was decorated for service in Korea and Vietnam, and self-published *Betrayed Trust* in 2004.

Nao Akutsu (1887–1947) was born in Nikko, Japan, and operated a shoe repair shop in Seattle with her husband, whom the Department of Justice interned as an enemy alien for two years. She was imprisoned at Puyallup and Minidoka with her sons, Jim and Gene, who both refused the draft on principle and served two years in federal prison. Spurned after the war by women in her church for her sons' actions, she took her own life.

Violet Kazue de Cristoforo (1917–2007) was a leading *haiku* poet, translator, and editor. Born in Ninole, Hawai'i, and educated in Japan, she was imprisoned in Fresno and Jerome before being segregated to Tule Lake. She renounced her citizenship and expatriated to Japan, but returned to California after the war and published six books and anthologies of poetry.

Brian Komei Dempster (b. 1969) is a Sansei poet and educator born in Seattle whose mother's family was imprisoned at Tanforan, Topaz, and Crystal City. He edited two volumes of workshop writing by former incarcerees, *From Our Side of the Fence* (2001) and *Making Home from War* (2011). His own poetry is collected in *Topaz* (2013) and *Seize* (2020).

Frank Emi (1916–2010) was a judo master born in Los Angeles and was running the family grocery when he was imprisoned at Pomona. At Heart Mountain he was one of seven leaders of the Fair Play Committee convicted of conspiracy to counsel draft evasion, and served eighteen months in prison. After the war he went to work for the U.S. Postal Service.

Bunyu Fujimura (1910–1997) was born in Gifu Prefecture, Japan, and became head minister of the Salinas Buddhist Temple in 1940. Arrested after Pearl Harbor, he was held in four Department of Justice internment camps before reuniting with his wife in Poston. He published his memoir *Though I Be Crushed* in 1985.

Lily Yuriko Nakai Havey (b. 1932) was ten years old when she was forcibly removed from Los Angeles to Santa Anita and Amache. At sixty-five, she began painting watercolors of her memories of camp and wrote vignettes to describe them, leading to her creative memoir, *Gasa Gasa Girl Goes to Camp* (2014).

Gordon K. Hirabayashi (1918–2012) was born in Seattle and was a senior at the University of Washington when he first refused to obey a military curfew that applied only to Japanese Americans, then refused to register for mass exclusion. He appealed his conviction for violating military orders to the Supreme Court; a federal appeals court vacated his conviction in 1987.

William Minoru Hohri (1927–2010) sued the U.S. government for $27 billion for wartime violations of civil and constitutional rights as lead plaintiff in a class-action lawsuit brought by his National Council for Japanese American Redress. Born in San Francisco, he was imprisoned at Manzanar at age fourteen.

Tatsuo Ryusei Inouye (1910–1999) was a judo master born in Laguna, California, and educated in Japan. He was imprisoned at Poston and segregated to Tule Lake, then held for three months without charge in the high-security stockade. After the war, he brought his family back to East Los Angeles, where he began a gardening service and resumed teaching judo out of his garage.

Ayako Ishigaki (1903–1996) was born in Tokyo and settled in New York City, where she wrote articles protesting Japan's rising militarism and published *Restless Wave* in 1940, one of the first memoirs in English by an Issei woman. She and her husband lived outside the exclusion zone and remained free during the war.

Shizue Iwatsuki (1896–1984) was an internationally recognized poet and Issei leader in Hood River, Oregon. Born in Okayama prefecture, Japan, she and her family were imprisoned at Pinedale, Tule Lake, and Minidoka. Her *tanka* are engraved in stone in Hood River and in Portland.

Bunichi Kagawa (1904–1981) was born in Yamaguchi prefecture, Japan, and studied at Stanford, where he published *Hidden Flame* (1930), one of the first books of poetry in English by an Issei. He was sent to Manzanar and segregated to Tule Lake, where he was the Issei mentor to the Kibei Nisei who founded and edited *Tessaku,* to which he contributed thirteen poems, five essays, and the introduction to the inaugural issue.

Hiroshi Kashiwagi (1922–2019) was a renowned poet and playwright, born in Sacramento and imprisoned at Marysville and Tule Lake. In San Francisco after the war he worked as a librarian, published *Shoe Box Plays* (2008), *Starting from Loomis and Other Stories* (2013), the memoir *Swimming in the American* (2005), and acted on stage and in films.

traci kato-kiriyama (b. 1973) is a Los Angeles poet and activist born in Harbor City to parents imprisoned as children at Manzanar and Tule Lake. Her poetry volumes are *signaling* (2010) and *Navigating With(out) Instruments* (2021). She is the principal writer of the multimedia play *Tales of Clamor.*

Kazuo Kawai (1921–1979) was born in Stockton, California, and educated in Japan. A voracious reader, he shared a passion for literature at Los Angeles Polytechnic High School with fellow Kibei Jōji Nozawa, and later worked for the *Sangyo Nippo,* a Japanese farm newspaper. At Poston, the questionnaire divided him from his mother, who preferred the freedoms of America, while Kawai sought expatriation. He was segregated to Tule Lake, where at twenty-three he helped found and edit *Tessaku*, in which he serialized his novel *The Age (Jidai)*, also translated as *These Times*, and published two poems and a short story. He lived for a time in Chicago after the war but eventually returned to California.

Iwao Kawakami (1907–1976) was born in Berkeley, California, and imprisoned at Tanforan and Topaz, where he worked on the *Topaz Times*. He married three times, once to poet Toyo Suyemoto, and served as sports editor for the *Nichi Bei Times*, which published his book, *The Parents and Other Poems*, in 1947.

Charles Kikuchi (1916–1988) was born in Vallejo, California, and kept a diary from Pearl Harbor through his departure from Tanforan for Gila River. He contributed his notes to the Japanese American Evacuation and Resettlement Study (JERS), for which he also interviewed fellow Nisei who had resettled in Chicago and wrote up their life histories for the JERS study, *The Salvage* (1952).

Christine Kitano (b. 1985) was born in Los Angeles, the daughter of Professor Harry Kitano of UCLA, who was imprisoned at Topaz. Her books of poetry are *Sky Country* (2017) and *Birds of Paradise* (2011), and she is co-editor of the oral history collection *Who You?: Hawai'i Issei* (2018) and *They Rise Like a Wave: An Anthology of Asian American Women Poets* (2022).

Henry (Yoshitaka) Kiyama (1885–1951) was born in Tottori prefecture, Japan, and came to study at the San Francisco Art Institute as a fine artist before turning to drawing a comic strip. In 1931 he self-published *The Four Immigrants Manga*, one of the first graphic novels in the United States, and returned to Japan before the war.

Fred Korematsu (1919–2005) defied the army's exclusion order in 1942 so that he could stay with his Italian American fiancée. He was arrested for violating military orders and bailed out to Tanforan and Topaz while his attorney appealed his conviction all the way to the Supreme Court. The discovery of evidence withheld from the court led a federal judge to vacate his conviction in 1983.

Joe Kurihara (1895–1965) was born on Kaua'i, Hawai'i, and fought with the U.S. Army in WWI. He was imprisoned at Manzanar where his speech to an already angry crowd set off a chain of events that led military police to fire into a crowd and kill two men. Kurihara was sent to the Moab and Leupp isolation centers and then to Tule Lake, where in protest he renounced his citizenship and expatriated to Japan; there, he translated for the U.S. Army.

Yoshito Kuromiya (1923–2018) was born in Sierra Madre, California, and imprisoned at Pomona and Heart Mountain, where he learned graphic design in the poster shop. He joined the Fair Play Committee and was among the sixty-three who were convicted of draft resistance, serving two years in a federal penitentiary. His *Beyond the Betrayal* (2021) is the only published memoir by a Nisei draft resister.

Mike Masaoka (1915–1991) led the decision as JACL national secretary and field executive to call for compliance with mass exclusion. Born in Fresno, California, and working from the JACL's wartime headquarters in Salt Lake City, he later urged the induction of the Nisei into the armed services as proof of loyalty, and was the first to volunteer.

Minoru Masuda (1915–1980) was born in Seattle and imprisoned at Puyallup and Minidoka, where he volunteered for the army. He was awarded the Bronze Star for service as a medic under fire with the 442nd RCT in Italy. Afterward, he taught psychology and behavioral sciences at the University of Washington and was a leader in the Seattle redress campaign.

Iwao Matsushita (1892–1979) was born in Hiroshima, Japan, and became a prominent businessman in Seattle, which led to his arrest and internment at Fort Missoula. After two years, he was finally able to reunite with his wife at Minidoka. After the war he became a student, teacher, and librarian at the University of Washington.

Janice Mirikitani (1941–2021) was a revolutionary artist born in Stockton, California, and imprisoned as a child at the Stockton Assembly Center and Rohwer. The author of five collections of poetry and editor of nine anthologies, she was San Francisco's second poet laureate and co-founder of the Glide Foundation, known as a citadel for social justice.

Perry Miyake (b. 1953) was born in Venice, California, to parents who returned to Venice and Gardena from Rohwer, Gila River, and

Tule Lake. He submitted the manuscript for his dystopian novel, *21st Century Manzanar* (2002), a week before the events of 9/11.

Toshio Mori (1910–1980), was born in Oakland, California, and published the first book of short stories by a Japanese American, *Yokohama, California*, which was delayed from 1942 to 1949 due to the war and anti-Japanese sentiment. He was imprisoned at Tanforan and Topaz. Rediscovery of his work late in his life led to the publication of his novel, *Woman from Hiroshima* (1978), and the collections *The Chauvinist and Other Stories* (1979) and *Unfinished Message* (2000).

David Mura (b. 1952) grew up in Chicago, where his parents resettled after their release from Jerome and Minidoka. He is the author of two memoirs, *Turning Japanese* (1991) and *Where the Body Meets Memory* (1995); a novel, *Famous Suicides of the Japanese Empire* (2008); and several collections of poetry.

Sada Murayama (1901–1995) was born in Yokosuka, Japan, and studied theater at the University of Washington. She directed Hiroshi Kashiwagi in The Little Theater at Tule Lake before her transfer to Jerome. At each camp she directed the USO chapter, and wrote a patriotic newspaper column.

Hiroshi Nakamura (1915–1973) was born in Gilroy, California, and imprisoned at Salinas, Poston, and Tule Lake, where he wrote *Treadmill*, the only novel written in English by a Japanese American about the incarceration as it was happening. It was published after his death when a microfilm copy was discovered in the National Archives.

Jōji Nozawa (1919–1983) was a Kibei born in Los Angeles and educated in Japan and at Los Angeles Polytechnic High School, where he met Kazuo Kawai. As George Joe Nozawa, he was imprisoned at Santa Anita and Amache and segregated to Tule Lake, where he helped found and edit *Tessaku*, in which he published five poems and three short stories. After the war he was a reporter and editor for the *Rafu Shimpo*, where he continued to publish the literary work of his fellow *Tessaku* writers. He also owned the Hakubun-Do gift shop, and became the exclusive U.S. import agent for National rice cookers, Zojirushi products, and Tokaido karate-gi.

John Okada (1923–1971) was born in Seattle and forcibly removed during his freshman year at the University of Washington to Puyallup and Minidoka. He later enlisted in the MIS, serving on Guam and in occupied Japan. He based his foundational 1957 novel, *No-No Boy*, on the draft resistance of Nao Akutsu's son, Hajime Jim Akutsu.

Hyakuissei Okamoto (dates unknown) was imprisoned at Stockton and Rohwer before being segregated to Tule Lake, where he joined with fellow poets to form a *haiku* collective that met monthly as the Tule Lake Valley Ginsha.

James Omura (1912–1994) was the lone Japanese American journalist to condemn the mass removal and JACL's advocacy of compliance. Born on Bainbridge Island, Washington, he voluntarily relocated from San Francisco to Denver, where he edited the *Rocky Shimpo* newspaper. He was tried alongside the Fair Play Committee steering committee for conspiracy to counsel draft evasion, but was acquitted.

Shelley Ayame Nishimura Ota (1911–1987) was born in Waiākea, Hawai'i, and later lived in Wisconsin. She wrote *Upon Their Shoulders* in 1948, the first novel by a Japanese American based on the story of Issei immigration and internment, but so soon after the war no publisher would take it, so she published it herself in 1951 and sold all five thousand copies.

Otokichi Ozaki (1904–1983) was a poet, editor, and Japanese language teacher born in Koichi prefecture, Japan, and was interned at six different camps before reuniting with his family at Jerome, from where they were all segregated to Tule Lake. He wrote thousands of *tanka* in tiny handwriting on thin rice paper to carry from camp to camp.

The **Portland senryū poets** of the *Bara Ginsha* group are **Masaki Kinoshita** as Jōnan (1896–1997), **Shigeru Mihara** as Goichi (1890–1960), **Taro Suenaga** as Sen Taro (1888–1947), **Masako Tomori** as Mokugyo (1913–1991), and **Shohei Tsuyuki** as Roshyou (1884–1945).

Brynn Saito (b. 1981) was born in Fresno, California. Her grandparents met and married at Gila River. A co-founder of the Yonsei Memory Project, she is the author of three books of poetry: *The Palace of Contemplating Departure* (2013), *Power Made Us Swoon* (2016), and *Under a Future Sky* (2023).

Jeanne Sakata (b. 1954) is a film, television and stage actress born in Watsonville, California. Her father was imprisoned at Poston. Her solo play inspired by the life of Gordon Hirabayashi, *Hold These Truths*, has been produced widely to great acclaim.

Shosuke Sasaki (1912–2002) was born in Yamaguchi prefecture, Japan, and imprisoned in Puyallup and Minidoka. While a statistician at Standard & Poor's in 1952, he stopped the New York Newspaper Guild from using the racial epithet "Jap." He was the Issei voice of the Seattle Evacuation Redress Committee.

Kiyo Sato (b. 1923) was born on a farm near Sacramento and imprisoned at age eighteen at Pinedale and Poston. She attained the rank of captain in the U.S. Air Force and worked as a public health nurse. Her memoir, *Kiyo's Story*, was published in 2009.

Tamotsu Shibutani (1920–2004) was a renowned sociologist born in Stockton, California, and imprisoned at Tanforan and Tule Lake, where as both incarceree and researcher he wrote field notes for the Japanese American Evacuation and Resettlement Study (JERS) that led to his 1966 publication of *Improvised News: A Sociological Study of Rumor*. His service with the MIS at Fort Snelling provided the basis for *The Derelicts of Company K* (1979).

Brandon Shimoda (b. 1978) is a Yonsei poet and educator born in Los Angeles with family members who were incarcerated at Heart Mountain and Poston. He wrote *The Grave on the Wall* (2019) after seeing photos of his grandfather in a barracks museum at Fort Missoula, Montana. His other books include *Hydra Medusa* (2023) and a forthcoming volume on the afterlife of incarceration.

Noboru Shirai (1907–1985) was born in Hiroshima, Japan, and was a graduate student in sociology at Stanford when he was imprisoned at Tule Lake, which he observed as both a WRA camp and segregation center. He wrote for *Tessaku* under the pen name of Chiyoda Manabu. After the war he was a correspondent for the *Nichi Bei Times* and president of Asahi Homecast, which provided Japanese radio and TV programs in Los Angeles.

Yasutaro Soga (1873–1957) was born in Tokyo and published the *Nippu Jiji* newspaper in Honolulu before his internment at Sand Island, Angel Island, Lordsburg, and Santa Fe, where he founded a *tanka* club. He published a memoir, *Tessaku Seikatsu* (*Life Behind Barbed Wire*), in 1948.

Monica Sone (1919–2011) was born Kazuko Itoi in Seattle and imprisoned at Puyallup and Minidoka. Her *Nisei Daughter* appeared in 1953 as the first memoir of incarceration from a woman's perspective. She had a long career in Ohio as a clinical psychologist and social worker.

Toyo Suyemoto (1916–2003) was born in Oroville, California, and recognized as a literary figure well before her imprisonment at Tanforan and Topaz, where she published poems in *All Aboard* and *TREK*. After the war she worked in libraries in Ohio. Her poems were rediscovered and published late in life, and her memoir, *I Call to Remembrance*, appeared posthumously in 2007.

Kentaro Takatsui (1915–2001) was born in Mukilteo, Washington, and studied at a Buddhist seminary in Tokyo. He was imprisoned at Puyallup and Tule Lake, where he led a movement to refuse to answer the loyalty questionnaire and was sent to WRA isolation centers at Moab and Leupp. In 1946 he enlisted to work as an MIS interpreter in occupied Japan, and later received top-secret clearance to serve in the army's Counter Intelligence Corps.

James Takeda (1915–1987) was born in Los Angeles and held at Santa Anita and Rohwer, where as the pipe-smoking co-editor of the *Rohwer Outpost* he wrote his Once Overs column. Nicknamed "Bean" for being as thin as a string bean, he worked after the war at his tax preparation business and as an interpreter for the Los Angeles Superior Court.

Fuyo Tanagi (1892–1989) was born in Fukushima, Japan. As the assistant editor of the *Hokubei Jiji* in Seattle she wrote and translated Japanese articles into English before her imprisonment at Puyallup and Minidoka, where she collected signatures on a petition protesting the drafting of Nisei men and rewrote the first draft written by Min Yasui with much stronger language.

Cherry Tanaka (1923–2008) was born in Seattle and imprisoned at Puyallup and Minidoka, where she co-edited the *Minidoka Irrigator* and wrote a column called Feminidoka. As Cherry Kinoshita, she fought for redress as president of the Seattle chapter of JACL and co-chaired the Washington Coalition for Redress.

Fujiwo Tanisaki (1921–2009) was born in Gallup, New Mexico, and educated in Japan. He was a young father in Los Angeles when he was forcibly removed to Manzanar, where he wrote poems and short stories, one of which he submitted to *Tessaku*. He later served with the Office of Strategic Services in India and occupied Japan, translating papers and interviewing civilians.

Kamekichi Tokita (1897–1948) was a leading artist in Seattle, where he operated a sign-painting business and managed a hotel while exhibiting his oil paintings nationally. Born in Shizuoka, Japan, he kept a diary starting on the night of Pearl Harbor up to the time of his family's forced removal to Puyallup, then resumed his diary and painting at Minidoka.

Amy Uyematsu (1947–2023) was a self-described "child of the antiwar, black power sixties," born in Pasadena, California, to parents who returned there from Manzanar and Gila River. Known for her essay "The Emergence of Yellow Power in America" (1971), she taught high school math and published six volumes of poetry.

Masae Wada (1903–1973) was born in Japan and was living in Santa Maria, California, when she was forcibly removed to Tulare and Gila River. An avid reader who was fond of reciting poetry, her "Gila Relocation Center Song" won a contest sponsored by the *Gila News-Courier*, whose reporter found it charming when Wada hesitated to have her name published.

Mitsuye Yamada (b. 1923) was born in Fukuoka, Japan, but was raised in Seattle and considers herself a Nisei. At both Puyallup and Minidoka, she took notes in writing tablets but put them away until finishing them for her 1976 collection, *Camp Notes and Other Poems*. Her recent work appears in *Full Circle: New and Selected Poems* (2019).

Eddie Yanagisako (1910–2002) and **Kenroku Sumida** (1912–1990) were both born in Hawai'i and worked at auto shops and fruit stands in Los Angeles before their imprisonment at Heart Mountain, where with the Fair Play Committee they each refused the draft and were sentenced to three years at the federal penitentiary in Leavenworth, Kansas.

Credits and Copyright Notices